The Historic Hotels of Spain

A Select Guide

WENDY ARNOLD

The Historic Hotels of Spain

A Select Guide

Photographs by
ROBIN MORRISON

CHRONICLE BOOKS
SAN FRANCISCO

For Bud and Barbara Munson
Remembering Chile's and New Hampshire's
eternal mountains

Frontispiece: looking up to the galleried double arcades from one of the peaceful courtyards of the Parador de Turismo de Almagro. See p. 75.

Opposite: a mouthwatering selection of local specialties at the Hotel La Bobadilla. See p. 91.

First published in the United States in 1991 by Chronicle Books.

Printed in Hong Kong

Library of Congress Cataloging-in-Publication Data available.

Arnold, Wendy.
    The historic hotels of Spain : a select guide / Wendy Arnold : photographs by Robin Morrison.
        p. cm.
      ISBN 0-87701-861-8
      1. Hotels, taverns, etc.—Spain—Guide-books. 2. Spain--Description and travel—1981—Guide-books. I. Title.
TX907.5.S7A76   1991
847.944601—dc20   90-20652
                                       CIP

Cover design by Julie Noyes

Map: Hanni Bailey

Distributed in Canada by
Raincoast Books
112 East Third Avenue
Vancouver, B.C. V5T 1C8

10 9 8 7 6 5 4 3 2 1

Chronicle Books
275 Fifth Street
San Francisco, California 94103

Contents

Preface

The Parador Nacional Raimundo de Borgoña stands in peaceful gardens just inside Avila's spectacular walls. See p. 45.

From the lush green hills and fields of Galicia in the northwest, through the central plains to the white-washed sun-baked Moorish villages of the far south, Spain is a land of contrasts. It is a land of high mountains, roaring rivers, and a variety of ancient and proud peoples each with their own regional language and customs. It was from Spain that Columbus sailed to discover the New World, and it was from Spain that the Conquistadors sailed to found an empire and to bring back the treasure of the Incas to Europe.

In medieval times, Santiago de Compostela ranked with Rome and Jerusalem as a place of pilgrimage, and millions came to visit it from all over Christendom. Many of the wonderful Romanesque churches which were built along the route are still there today, as are the monasteries built to house the pilgrims. Even then, castles dominated every crag rising from the plains, guarded every mountain pass, and towered above every ancient city. Now, these battlemented castles and cloistered monasteries, together with magnificent mansions, age-old beamed farmhouses, and sophisticated *belle-époque* extravaganzas are a luxurious and enjoyable treasury of historic hotels.

It has been twenty years since I first explored Spain. Then, prices were low but roads sometimes uneven and accommodation often unremarkable. The changes have impressed me beyond measure. Now, road surfaces are good, charming old hotels have been splendidly refurbished, and new hotels created from picturesque buildings. Understandably, prices have also risen dramatically. In Spain, as in most places, you get what you pay for, and high-quality food and service are expensive.

Staying in Spanish paradors is fascinating. The government has rescued wonderful historic castles and mansions and employed gifted architects to transform them into comfortable hotels with excellent modern amenities without in the least losing their atmosphere and character. They are warm in the winter, cool in summer, and provide an excellent choice of food, always with optional local specialties and regional wines. In remote scenic areas which have no suitable existing buildings to convert, modern paradors have been built. All are worth a visit.

I have ignored the often disastrous modern coastal resorts and sought out hotels of character and charm in Spain's most interesting areas. I have favored hotels where desk-staff will take your messages reliably, where showers work efficiently, and which I felt were the best in the area, even if the cuisine left something to be desired. I have noted those with particularly fine tables. I have also noted exactly and truthfully what I have found. I hope that in this way guests and hotels can match up accurately and happily, fulfilling each other's expectations. I never accept any hospitality or favors from a hotel, or let them know what I am doing until after I have paid my bill.

Anyone who until now has only stayed on the coast should explore some of the inland areas, perhaps following one of the pilgrim roads or going up into one of the mountain nature reserves. Spain is a fine country for sportsmen and river fishing. Galicia and Catalonia are especially captivating – I was amazed by the variety and profusion of the wildflowers that covered the countryside in the spring.

Hotel managers in Spain are rarely visible – not unexpectedly, those hotels with the greatest sparkle and polish were those where I found the manager most deeply involved in the day-to-day running of the hotel and interested in meeting guests and hearing their thoughts.

There is talk of the Spanish government selling off the paradors as private hotels. Should this happen, it would be a splendid opportunity to own your own luxurious but amazingly picturesque castle in Spain.

General Information

Preparation It is *always* best to make reservations in advance. Visit or contact your nearest Spanish Tourist Office for brochures on Spain's many different regions. Try to avoid the crushing August heat in southern Spain. Tourism peaks during Easter week fiestas, so avoid that week or make reservations early; just before or after is good. Most Spanish towns and villages have at least one noisy yearly fiesta – inquire when you make reservations. Write to reserve hotels well in advance and be sure to inquire about the availability of king-sized beds. (European double beds are cozily narrow: rooms with twin beds are usually larger.) Clearly specify the type of bed, preferred view, and request the exact price plus tax and service charges; confirm your reservation and prices by letter. En route ask your present hotel to phone ahead to your next hotel to confirm your room and arrival time – calculate your arrival time generously. When planning sight-seeing note that even cathedrals close from 1:00–4:00 pm and museums may be closed on Mondays. Lunch in hotels is served until 2:00–3:00 pm and dinner is rarely served before 9:00 pm, except in paradors. (If ordering from room service, check prices first to avoid shocks.)

Getting There Before driving in Spain *always* have an international driving license, bail-bond (unique in Europe but essential unless you want to sample a Spanish jail), and medical insurance. Freeways are few and toll-paying, but worth every peseta. On all but the twisting northern freeways you can average a legal 120km per hour out of season. Other main roads have good surfaces. Many are currently being widened, but most are narrow and heavily traveled by trucks, so pass with care. On hills watch out for cars passing on curves and crawler lanes that end at the hilltop with little warning. Estimate average speed as 45km per hour. Avoid big cities in rush hours; triple parking is common. Sundays and siesta times are best. Signposting is excellent out of town, but difficult to spot in town. Before leaving, buy detailed maps showing regional variations of place-names. (Michelin's orange *Cartes Routières et Touristiques* are good.) Remember that gas stations on side roads may not accept credit cards, so carry enough cash to cover that day's driving expenses. Avoid roads not on the map as they may turn into goat tracks. Avoid driving across France on the 1st and 30th of August, the 14th of July, and the second week in September as those days are holidays. Flights to and within Spain are reasonable and often have fly/drive options.

Food and Drink Try *tapas* bars for tiny plates of finger food, from local almonds to regional delicacies, with your wine or beer. Where the locals eat is usually better than tourist places, and a complete dinner menu is better value than à la carte. In paradors sample regional menus. Note hotels where I have specifically commended the food; at others consider room service snacks or eating out. Spanish food is robust but not usually spicy. Drink mineral water. It is worth making the effort to come down to breakfast – buffets offer lavish choices.

Paradors Obtain a complete list of paradors from the tourist office. Government owned and run hotels, though *not* cheap, they are often in historic buildings (some are in modern buildings). They are a good option for non-Spanish speakers making a first trip to Spain as they are delightfully decorated with local fabrics, traditional tiles, wrought-iron work, and antiques. They are clean, efficient, and reliable; with luxury bathrooms and good beds. They are often in remote mountainous regions with no comparable accommodation. Their staff is well-trained and polite and rather serious. Guests are of mixed nationalities, including Spanish. Paradors have a 3–4 star national rating. I was delighted to find the staff astonished if I tipped.

Terms I have divided hotels into broad categories, based on two people sharing a double room for one night, and breakfast, but *not* including government tax, service, other meals, drinks, or phone calls. NB Expect astronomic minibar/phone call prices.

Moderate	9,300–13,800 ptas	($96–142)
Expensive	14,300–17,800 ptas	($147–183)
Deluxe	18,000–26,500 ptas	($187–273)
Super-deluxe	31,500–50,000 ptas	($324–515)

Exchange rate: 180 ptas = $1.95

Bullfighting Before deciding to attend, pause to think that the object is to kill the bulls, as stylishly as possible, and that people also sometimes get killed. This is not a quaintly pretty tourist entertainment.

Footnote The Spanish are an extremely courteous race and appreciate this quality in others, though unhappy experiences with foreigners may have embittered locals in mass-tourism towns. As everywhere else in the world, take the sensible precaution of not leaving valuables in hotel rooms, keeping wallets in buttoned pockets or closed purses, not flaunting valuable jewelry, and never leaving anything visible in parked cars. An enclosed overnight parking place is a good investment. Off the beaten tourist track, or in smaller hotels, you will probably find only Spanish spoken.

BAY

OF

BISCAY

N

④ ⑥
④ 🏛 🏛 ③
Santander *Bilbao* 🏛 ①

⑧ 🏛 🏛 ⑦
⑨ 🏛 ⑰ 🏛 ⑱
Santiago de 🏛 ⑤ ⑲ 🏛
Compostela *León* 🏛 ② ⑳ 🏛
🏛 ⑩ *Burgos*
⑪ 🏛 ㉑ 🏛
⑫ 🏛 *Barcelona*

PORTUGAL

㉒ 🏛

⑬ 🏛 ⑭ 🏛 ⑮
Madrid 🏛 ⑯

㉓ 🏛

S P A I N *Valencia*

🏛 ㉔

Córdoba

🏛 ㉖ 🏛 ㉕
㉗ 🏛 🏛 ㉘ 🏛 ㉚
Seville ㉙ 🏛 *Granada*

Cadiz *Malaga* *MEDITERRANEAN SEA*

0   300 MIs
0   250Km

Belle-époque charm

A full-length portrait of Queen María Cristina of Spain, elegant in a long black gown, hangs in the pillared entrance hall of this gracious *belle-époque* hotel. Built in 1912, and designed by Charles Mewes, the architect of the Ritz hotels in Paris, Madrid, and London, the María Cristina has a graceful staircase, large, well-equipped bedrooms, and a splendidly elaborate restaurant. Refurbished throughout, it has been fully airconditioned and its period bathrooms have been brought up to date, adding modern comfort to the hotel's gilded charm.

After driving down beside the river, follow the signs to the hotel's main entrance under a striped awning, overlooking gardens and palm trees. A porter hurries out to greet you and check-in is swift and efficient. My large blue-carpeted bedroom was lit by brass chandeliers and still retained its original fitted mahogany closets inlaid with the hotel's crowned crest. TV and minibar were discreetly concealed in a tallboy. The bed's soft linen sheets and big down pillows provided a comfortable night's sleep. Breakfast was set out on a well-starched damask cloth, with a rose in a silver vase. Sugary buns, croissants, fruit compote, toast, assorted preserves, and coffee were all excellent.

I also enjoyed eating in the hotel restaurant, where service was polished and the food well-presented and expertly cooked. From a choice of both international and local dishes, I selected shrimps cooked in garlic butter, squid in its own ink, and a passionfruit sorbet. The area is known for its seafood – fishing boats have sailed from San Sebastián to as far as Newfoundland and Greenland since medieval times.

The local people are Basques, thought to be the original inhabitants of the Iberian peninsula. They still preserve their own distinct language and culture which has imbued them with a burning desire for autonomy. (Be sure to have a map giving both the Spanish and the Basque version of place names. San Sebastián's local name, for instance, is Donostia.)

San Sebastián is a popular resort – the kings of Spain used to spend summers here – and lies along the perfectly curved La Concha bay. The wide, sandy beach is edged with a fashionable promenade, and both are crowded in summer. The bay's mouth is guarded by a craggy islet and dominated by the peak of Monte Urgull.

The city celebrates many festivals: that of its patron saint in January with drums and bands, costumes and parades; the summer solstice, with rites dating back to pagan times; horse racing season; and traditional Basque trials of strength and expertise, including boat races on the bay, weight lifting, and pelota matches. The year ends with a film festival said to rival that of Cannes and a December gastronomic fair. Check dates of the festivities with the hotel when booking, in order to attend or to avoid them.

The splendors of this turn-of-the-century hotel include a colonnaded restaurant (opposite) and a gracious spiraling staircase (above).

HOTEL MARÍA CRISTINA, paseo República Argentina 4, 20004 San Sebastián/Donostia. **Tel.** (43) 42 49 00; (43) 42 67 70 (reservations). **Telex** 38195. **Fax** (43) 42 39 14. **Owners** Soc. Fomento de San Sebastián, S.A. **Managing Company** Cigahotels. **General Manager** D. Ramón Felip. **Open** All year. **Rooms** 139 (incl. 17 junior, 13 grand suites), all with bathroom (incl. wall shower), direct-dial phone, TV, radio, minibar, airconditioning, room service, laundry. **Facilities** Hall-promenade, bar, restaurant, elevators, airconditioning, 6 reception/conference rooms with audio-visual/secretarial/simultaneous translation services by arrangement. Nearby beach/swimming/sailing/fishing; golf 18km, tennis 2km. **Restrictions** No dogs. **Terms** Deluxe. **Credit cards** Visa, Amex, Diners, Air Plus. **Closed parking** 50 spaces reserved nearby, paying. **Getting there** Madrid 488km via N I/A I/A 8. Motorway exit 7, follow W. bank of river, hotel signposted on L. Nearest int. airports, Biarritz, France 53km/Bilbao 104km, both by motorway. **Of local interest** Town; aquarium, parks, port; Fuenterrabía/Hondarribia (parador El Emperador); Pasajes de San Juan/Pasai Donibane. **Whole day expeditions** Guetaría/Getaria; Zumaya/Zumaia; Motrico/Mutricu. **Eating out** Arzak, Akelarre, etc. Ask at hotel.

Among the wheatfields

A swirl of white doves flew up to their dovecote by the gate as I drove into the courtyard of the Landa Palace Hotel. With its farm carts and ornamental bandstand, it looks like some little village square. This is a bustling, popular eating place for locals and tourists alike, with a menu in three languages including English, a large bar with a tiled corner fireplace, and a lunchtime restaurant enlivened by red-checked tablecloths and rustic antiques. Some dishes arrive sizzling on cast-iron platters; a boy in peasant costume offers a vast selection of breads (baked in a wood-fired oven) from a huge, flat wicker basket; and the house specialty – whole roast leg of milk-fed lamb – carved up between two people at the table is served with generous helpings of potatoes. If peasant fare does not appeal, pick a more delicate dish with confidence – the head chef trained at some of the finest French 3-star Michelin establishments. Sample wine from nearby Rioja vineyards. Dinner is by candle-light under soaring stone arches in the evening restaurant.

Do not miss a swim in the indoor/outdoor pool – during my stay it was ornamented with floating bouquets of flowers. You can see the wheatfields through its intricate windows – the hotel's stonework was carved by a mason who for many years also worked on the restoration of Burgos's great Gothic cathedral, one of the finest in Spain.

The city lies on the medieval pilgrim road to Santiago de Compostela and has a wealth of historic buildings: for instance, the convent of Las Huelgas, its chapel rich in royal tombs, which was once ruled by abbesses whose power was second only to that of the queen. Some miles to the south-east is the monastery of Santo Domingo de Silos. Outstanding Romanesque carvings can be found in its two-story cloister.

The hotel's square tower dates from the 14th century. It was moved from its original site and rebuilt here, and the rest of the hotel was added in traditional style using ancient beams and stones. The family has filled it with pieces of antique furniture and their own collections of clocks, cradles, and ceramics.

Bedrooms have no minibars, as the hotel prides itself on swift and efficient room service. My excellent breakfast did indeed arrive rapidly, and was attractively served on patterned blue china. Specifically request one of the newly refurbished bedrooms with a four-poster, pretty sprigged cotton furnishings, antique-style modern bathroom, huge closets, and views over the countryside to the cathedral's distant spires. Looking out, you may see as I did a formation of migrating storks with wide, black-tipped wings flying over, or watch a shepherd and his dog patiently following a small herd of sheep over the brown winter fields.

Opposite: an evening swim in the scenic pool is followed by a candlelit dinner and the comfort of a four-poster bed. Fascinating collections of objects are displayed around the hotel, such as the pottery jars (above) and the forecourt's antique farmcarts (overleaf).

LANDA PALACE HOTEL, carretera Madrid-Irún, Km 236, Burgos. **Tel.** (47) 20 63 43. **Telex** 39534. **Fax** (47) 26 46 76. **Owners** Landa family. **Manager** Sra Victoria Landa. **Open** All year. **Rooms** 42, all with bathroom (incl. wall shower), direct-dial phone, TV, 24-hr. room service. **Facilities** Several salons, bar, 2 restaurants, elevator, airconditioning, indoor/outdoor pool, gardens, 2 conference rooms. **Restrictions** No dogs. **Terms** Deluxe. **Credit cards** Visa, Eurocard/Mastercard only. **Closed parking** Underground, paying. **Getting there** Madrid 236.5km. On Burgos-Madrid road 3.5km from town. Nearest int. airport, Bilbao, 156km. **Of local interest** Cathedral and churches; Casa del Cordón; convent of Las Huelgas (royal tombs, cloisters, chapel, etc.); Hospital del Rey; charterhouse of Miraflores (royal tombs); local folkloric and religious festivals – ask at hotel. **Whole day expeditions** Sto Domingo de Silos (Romanesque cloister, museum); pilgrim road to Sto Domingo de la Calzada (parador); Rioja vineyards round Haro. **Eating out** Casa Ojeda, Mesón del Cid.

In a fashionable resort

The Hotel Real is about three kilometers from the port in Santander, in the pleasant beach resort area of El Sardinero. A handsome, white-painted building, perched high on a hillside, its bedrooms have tranquil sea views. Built early in the 20th century, it is the quintessential dignified grand hotel by the sea. You walk up a flight of steps into a glassed-in seating area, and down a long, polished parquet-floored hall, where once guests used to promenade for exercise in rainy weather, to the reception desk on the right. Arched glass doors lead into a salon ornamented with plasterwork swags and gleaming chandeliers. Armchairs are arranged among palm trees in conversation groups; frilled floral chintz frames the seascape. At one end of the salon is a mirrored bar with cool green decor, at the other the winter restaurant. In summer guests often eat on the enclosed terrace which is airconditioned, like the rest of the hotel.

My meal was delicious, attentively served by friendly girls at a table spread with white damask and decorated with a pretty arrangement of fresh flowers. An old-fashioned garlic and bread soup was based on an excellent stock; another traditional local dish, hake, served with a green herb sauce, was equally good, the fish sparklingly fresh and cooked to tender translucence, the sauce subtle and light. The selection of desserts looked so inviting that I indulged myself with a chocolate gateau. All the cheeses on the cheese board were locally produced and in prime condition.

The hotel was being redecorated floor by floor while I was there. The fifth floor at the top, which naturally has the best views, and can be reached by elevator, has been specially refurbished with executives in mind. Bathrobes, hairdriers, and excellent showers are provided in the luxurious brown marble and tiled modern bathrooms. Baskets of fruit await guests in the bedrooms, which have their original handsome mahogany furniture, as well as minibar, touch-dial phone, fitted carpets, and pleasing decor.

From the balconies of the lower-floor rooms, you can look out over the terraces, palms, rose bushes, and white ornamental garden furniture in the well-tended grounds, and even catch a glimpse of the sea between the trees. The decor is simpler – room rates are also more modest. Request a sea view.

For those based in England who wish to bring over their own car, the 24-hour crossing by boat from Plymouth to Santander across the Bay of Biscay may appeal more than the long drive across France, and non-Spanish speakers may appreciate having the ferry company plan an itinerary and book ahead.

Opposite above: the view from the bedrooms of the curving bay is spectacular; the chandelier-hung salon (opposite below) and the winter restaurant (above) are gracious and comfortable.

HOTEL REAL, paseo Pérez Galdós 28, 39005 Santander, Cantabria. **Tel.** (42) 27 25 50. **Telex** 39012. **Fax** (42) 27 45 73. **Owners** Grupo Hoteles Unidos S.A. **Manager** D. Carlos García Rodriguez. **Open** All year. **Rooms** 125 (incl. 15 suites), all with bathroom (incl. wall shower), direct-dial phone, TV with satellite and video channels, radio, minibar, airconditioning, terrace/balcony, room service, laundry. **Facilities** Salon, bar, restaurant, elevators, airconditioning, gardens, 7 conference rooms. Audio-visual/ secretarial / simultaneous translation / photographer / self-drive/chauffeured cars by arrangement. Nearby beach/ sailing/surfing/fishing. Golf 20km, tennis 1km. **Restrictions** No dogs. **Terms** Expensive. **Credit cards** All major. **Closed parking** Yes, free. **Getting there** Madrid 393km; drive through town dir. El Sardinero, turn L up coast, hotel on L up hill. Local airport 10km. By boat (24 hrs): Brittany Ferries, Plymouth (0752) 221321 (crossing); (0752) 263388 (holidays). **Of local interest** Altamira caves (appointment only); Santillana del Mar (see p. 19); beaches; town; casino. **Whole day expeditions** E. along coast to Castro-Urdiales via Noja, Santoña, Laredo; W. to San Vicente de la Barquera; SW. to Picos de Europa mountains (modern parador at Fuente Dé). **Eating out** Cañadio, La Posada del Mar, El Puerto, Zacarías, Mesón Segoviano, El Molino, etc.

In a perfect medieval village

Thirty-five years ago the cruise liner on which I was traveling to South America called in at Santander, and I went to visit the cave paintings at Altamira – an experience I have never forgotten. Lunch at the Parador Gil Blas in historic Santillana del Mar followed. I always promised myself to return one day.

You must now apply many months in advance to view the caves, as entry is very restricted. Visitors came in such numbers that they altered the humidity and temperature levels in the caves and the paintings began to deteriorate. But you can wander at will in Santillana del Mar, said to be the most beautiful small town in Spain. By some quirk of fate its cobbled medieval streets have survived the centuries unspoilt. Some of its picturesque houses were built when this was the medieval capital of the province of Asturias, others added by wealthy nobles returning with their riches from South America – houses bear their stone escutcheons. Balconies are bright with flowers, while green fields around provide a peaceful setting. The town is named for Santa Illiana, or Juliana, buried here in the 6th century AD. It gained further fame as the birthplace of the fictional 17th-century hero Gil Blas, for whom the parador is named, and whose creator never in fact visited Spain.

In season the town is crammed with tourists, so if you want to see it at its best, visit the surrounding area during the day, then return at night to the simply furnished rooms at the parador, with their polished floorboards and high ceilings, and walk through the now quiet, lamplit streets.

The Parador Gil Blas is a picturesque 15th-century mansion. Its solid wooden door faces the tiny main square – the entry hall is paved with patterned pebbles and furnished with massive antiques. A tapestry-hung wooden stairway leads up past a suit of armor to a salon with hand-hewn beams, and quiet, spacious bedrooms with good modern bathrooms.

Downstairs is a convivial small bar and a large dining room lit by brass chandeliers. Wild asparagus in a light cheese sauce, lamb stew, and apple pie were all good, and the breakfast buffet next morning was heaped high with different breads, cakes, fruits, and sausages. The girls serving at table were polite and efficient.

Those wishing for hotel-style sophistication may wish to stay in nearby Santander (see p. 17), though they must disregard the ugly industrial area that lies between the towns. But if you choose the parador you will wake to the sound of cocks crowing, and open the wooden shutters on a quiet garden, local farmers setting off for a day in the fields, and the sun rising over ancient, tiled roofs.

Guests enter from the cobbled village square directly into the parador's beamed entrance hall (opposite). The balcony above the main entrance is bright with flags and flowers (above).

PARADOR NACIONAL GIL BLAS, plaza Ramón Pelayo 11, 39330 Santillana del Mar, Santander, Cantabria. **Tel.** (42) 81 80 00. **Fax** (42) 81 83 91. **Owners** Spanish Government. **Manager** Juan Mª Garralda Iribarren. **Open** All year. **Rooms** 28 in main building, 28 in annex, all with bathroom, direct-dial phone, TV, radio, minibar. **Facilities** 3 bars, restaurant, airconditioning in annex, garden, 3 conference rooms. **Restrictions** No dogs in restaurant. **Terms** Moderate. **Closed parking** Yes, paying. **Getting there** Madrid 393km; from W., signposted L off main Santander road. From E., via Santander, about 37km further W. Brittany Ferries: Plymouth (0752) 221321 (crossing); (0752) 263388 (holidays). **Of local interest** Explore town, 12th-C. church, museum in 17th-C. convent; beaches Playa Comillas, Playa de Oyambre; for Altamira caves, apply many months in advance to Centro de Investigación de Altamira, Santillana del Mar, Santander, or ask on arrival about cancellations. **Whole day expeditions** San Vicente de la Barquera; Picos de Europa mountains (modern parador at Fuente Dé). **Eating out** Only small local places, ask at parador.

Monastic splendor

A town stood on the site of León before the coming of the Romans. Their Seventh Legion made a fortified camp here in 70 AD beside the Bernesga river to guard the surrounding plains. Waves of Vandals, Iberians, and finally Moors destroyed and rebuilt the town, until eventually it was retaken by Christian armies early in the 10th century. It became a base for the reconquest of Castile and the most important town in this part of Spain. In the 12th century, Augustinian monks founded a monastery on the riverbank where a bridge crossed the water, to lodge "the poor of Christ" who were following the pilgrim route to Santiago de Compostela. From here the military order of the Knights of St. James patrolled the roads and protected wayfarers. The monastery, magnificently rebuilt in the 16th century, is now a hotel, which continues to shelter travelers but provides them with today's comforts.

The hotel's façade is richly embellished with busts of saints, monarchs, and heroes from mythology and history – Hercules; King Ferdinand and Queen Isabella, patrons of Columbus's voyage of discovery; St. James vanquishing the Moors. Massive plate-glass doors open into a great stone hall, from which a monumental stone stairway leads up to a few enormous suites of high-ceilinged rooms with carved and painted antique furniture. Most guests stay in the rather more modest modern rooms, leading from cream marble corridors, that have been added to the back of the building. Although small, the bedrooms are pleasantly furnished with solid wooden furniture, carved wooden doors, wrought-iron fittings, and good modern marble bathrooms. They are snugly heated in winter and airconditioned in summer. The sheets are silky-soft sea-island cotton – I requested and was given a bedboard for my too yielding bed.

The public rooms are huge, roofed with gigantic beams, hung with tapestries, and overlooking inner courtyards. From the entrance hall you can see into the peaceful garden cloisters of the attached church, which can be visited by arrangement; its museum has

many treasures, including an 11th-century ivory figure of Christ.

Until fairly recently the San Marcos was an independent hotel which had sadly become run down. Now state owned, it is being splendidly restored and refurbished, so specify when booking that you wish to have a refurbished room. The menu is being revised to improve the former rather bland mid-Atlantic fare, and to provide a more tempting alternative to the excellent eating places in the town.

Parts of the old city walls still stand. Near them is the Basilica of San Isidoro, which has some strikingly fine Romanesque paintings and royal tombs. Town parking is difficult and you may prefer to walk in or take a taxi rather than move your car from the enclosed parking behind the hotel. In winter take advantage of Spain's late lunchtime to go sightseeing in the morning, since everything shuts from 1 to 4pm, after which it will be too dark to enjoy the beauty of the stained glass windows of the cathedral, whose glory rivals that of Chartres.

Tranquil, cloistered gardens (opposite), fine antiques (above), and an imposing façade, majestic staircase, and soaring Gothic chapel (all overleaf) make staying here an unforgettable experience.

HOTEL DE SAN MARCOS, plaza de San Marcos 7, 24001 León. **Tel.** (87) 23 73 00. **Telex** 89809. **Fax** (87) 23 34 58. **Owners** Spanish Government. **Manager** César Alvarez Montoto. **Open** All year. **Rooms** 256, all with bathroom (incl. wall shower), direct-dial phone, TV, radio. **Facilities** Salon, bar, restaurant, elevators, airconditioning, garden, 6 conference rooms. **Restrictions** No dogs. **Terms** Expensive. **Credit cards** All major. **Closed parking** Yes, free.

Getting there Madrid 327km via N VI–N 630. Hotel is beside river, signposted in town. **Of local interest** Church attached to parador; cathedral; Basilica of San Isidoro; town. **Whole day expeditions** San Miguel de Escalada, Villarmún church; Astorga cathedral and museum, archbishop's palace by Gaudí, churches, town walls. **Eating out** Independencia, Bitácora, Mesón Leones del Racimo de Oro.

An architectural gem

A vast stone coat of arms dominates the main entrance of the Hotel de la Reconquista, a magnificent 18th-century building named for the reconquest of Spain by Christian forces from the Moors. These had swept up unchecked from the south and through Castile until finally halted in 718 AD at nearby Covadonga.

The hotel was originally built as an orphanage in the 1750s. Its magnificent public rooms are arranged around a series of arcaded and balconied courtyards, all open, except the first, which is roofed over into an immense salon. A smaller inner court, known intriguingly as "Patio de los Gatos," "Courtyard of the Cats," is stone-pillared and arcaded. This imposing hotel stands at the heart of the city, just to the north of the large central square – the Parque de San Francisco. If you arrive early enough to park on the hotel's forecourt, your car should be perfectly safe – the town's main police station is just opposite.

Oviedo is a large manufacturing city. Companies find the hotel a convenient venue for meetings and conferences, and its high-ceilinged chapel is popular for elaborate society weddings. Tourists appreciate its central position surrounded by high-quality shops and within walking distance of the old city and cathedral. It became a hotel in the early 1970s; some of the smaller bedrooms still retain the space-age decor favored at that time – specify if you would prefer a larger bedroom furnished with antiques. All are equipped with airconditioning and a TV with English-language channels, and enjoy 24-hour room service. The hotel has its own arcade of luxury boutiques, a beauty shop, and a convenient coffee shop as well as a restaurant. An excellent assortment of eating places, some Michelin starred, are close at hand.

My pink-walled, close-carpeted bedroom had a comfortable bed with well-positioned reading lamp, a desk running the width of the room, comprehensive minibar, and large armchair upholstered in corduroy with a matching davenport. There was an extensive

range of fitted closets, an extra phone, and a high-tech shower in the bathroom. Breakfast was excellent, with a delicious selection of freshly baked breads and pastries.

The Parador Nacional Molino Viejo twenty-eight kilometers away on the coast at Gijón is modern, but based on an old windmill, and in a park. You can drop in for lunch – sample local cider. There are fishing villages nearby to explore. The coastline is ruggedly beautiful, and inland there is the natural grandeur of the Picos de Europa mountains, with their wild flowers and picturesque villages.

Asturias is a pleasant province; its ancient farmhouses have distinctive traditional granaries, whose overhanging eaves are festooned with braided golden corncobs. You occasionally still see a farm cart drawn by oxen.

Stately elegance is found in the galleried salon and bedroom (opposite: top and bottom right), and 18th-century magnificence in the domed chapel (opposite bottom left, and above).

HOTEL DE LA RECONQUISTA, Gil de Jaz 16, 33004 Oviedo. **Tel.** (85) 24 11 00. **Telex** 84328. **Fax** (85) 24 11 66. **Owners** H.O.A.S.A. **Managing company** Cigahotels. **General Manager** D. Pedro Lozano. **Open** All year. **Rooms** 142 (incl. 6 junior suites, 5 suites), all with bathroom (incl. wall shower and hairdrier), direct-dial phone, TV with English-language channel, radio, minibar, airconditioning, laundry. **Facilities** Salon, bar, restaurant, coffee shop, beauty shop, shopping arcade, sauna, 10 conference rooms, audio-visual/secretarial/simultaneous translation/photocopying/photographer by arrangement. **Restrictions** None. **Terms** Deluxe. **Credit cards** All major. **Closed parking** Yes, paying. **Getting there** Madrid 443km. Local airport 47km. Hotel in town center. **Of local interest** Old city and cathedral; Cuesta de Naranco hill with 9th-C. churches; Gijón with Parador Molino Viejo and park. **Whole day expeditions** Coastal villages Luanco, Avilés, Salinas, Pravia, Cudillero. **Eating out** Casa Fermín, Trascorrales, El Raitan.

A mountain retreat

Everyone looked surprised when I arrived at La Rectoral. It seems that foreign tourists seldom make their way up to this remote village just over the border into Asturias. If you go via Ribadeo you will travel the scenic coast road, which climbs up and down amid woodland and sometimes spectacular sea vistas. At Ribadeo I had called in at the modern parador which had a large tank of live lobsters in the restaurant, and offered a promising seafood menu and lovely views over the bay – request a top-floor room if you decide to stay there, as some lower bedrooms have no view.

I picked a back road which led to Taramundi along a series of hairpin bends with no safety barriers. The views were impressive, over lush green pastures and small, rustic farmhouses. When I left, I discovered a less challenging route via Mousende which joined the main Lugo-Ribadeo road, had proper markings and edges, and crossed and recrossed the River Eo, the boundary between Galicia and Asturias – a better road for the timorous.

Taramundi has a most picturesque foothill setting; the scenery alone is worth the journey. The hotel, once a rectory, is a quaint 18th-century stone, slate, and wooden building, set into the hillside above the village, up a very steep drive. The barn has been transformed into a salon, and there is a small bar with a pleasingly uneven wooden floor, and a shuttered dining room which looks out over the slopes. The bedrooms are in a modern addition, behind a traditional, many-paned tall window, typical of Asturias, which resembles the stern window of a Spanish galleon. Lower-floor rooms have small, flower-decked, open-air terraces, though all rooms have indoor terraces behind the glass, where you can sit and admire the scenery, closed off from the room by a sliding mirrored door. This is a very good place to breakfast, as I did, watching the sun come up over the mountains.

The rooms are modern, with thick, woven Spanish bedcovers, couch, airconditioning, and TV. The up-to-date, tiled bathrooms have gold-plated taps. There is a small downstairs gymnasium with a window revealing the bedrock from which it has been excavated. The food is unpretentious – I sampled a good vegetable soup and breaded veal cutlet.

The hotel also owns some small, three-bedroomed, 18th-century cottages with full modern comforts, but featuring open hearths, and with maid service. These sounded promising, but as they were all occupied, I could not see them.

I liked this friendly little hotel, and enjoyed sitting before dinner discussing with the barman the merits of the different local liqueurs. These are made from the herbs and wildflowers which in spring carpet the surrounding meadows. The liqueur called "pacharan" was particularly good. All the staff were courteous and helpful, as was the man at the filling station from whom I asked directions, though not everyone spoke English this far from the tourist tracks. I was pleased to have discovered a mountain retreat where most of my fellow-guests were Spanish, and which was in such a fascinating, ancient Asturian house.

Opposite: distant views from a bedroom window across flower-filled meadows complement the hotel's rustic charm. Above: a corner of the shuttered dining room.

LA RECTORAL, 33775 Taramundi, Asturias. **Tel.** (85) 63 40 60. **Owners** D.I.T.A.S.A. **Manager** Jesus Mier Barrenechea. **Open** All year, except Jan.–Feb. **Rooms** 12, all with bathroom (incl. wall shower), direct-dial phone, TV, radio, minibar, airconditioning. Also cottages. **Facilities** Salon, bar, restaurant, garden, gymnasium. Riding/fishing by arrangement. **Restrictions** No dogs. **Terms** Moderate.

Credit cards Amex, Visa, Diners. **Closed parking** No. **Getting there** Madrid 571km via N VI, turning off at Lugo on Ribadeo road, R at Pontenova-Villaodriz, 9km via Conforto/Mousende. **Of local interest** Local rural handicrafts, incl. pottery, carvings, fabrics; fishing/riding by arrangement. **Whole day expeditions** Walks and drives, ask at hotel. **Eating out** No.

A friendly tower stronghold

I found this parador – a massive octagonal tower with walls eight feet thick – most intriguing. Historians cannot agree whether it dates originally from the 11th or 13th centuries; it was restored in 1480. Of the once great fortress, now only this, the Andrade Tower, remains, and the small, bustling town totally encircles it. You enter across a dry moat, under the pointed teeth of a great iron portcullis, through a door high in the tower. The main hall has comfortable chairs, painted scenes from the history of the castle, and lights set in great wrought-iron and yellow glass flambeaux.

Upstairs there are only six bedrooms, reached by a small elevator or a sturdy wooden staircase ornamented with plants in antique earthenware pots. Each bedroom is large; mine had a deep alcove in the immensely thick walls, with a window seat and a tiny window looking out over the countryside. There was a granite fireplace, a low-beamed ceiling, ancient yellow velvet easy chairs, a desk, an antique mirror, and a carved and gilded chest inlaid with ivory incised with depictions of people, flowers, and animals. Pleasant watercolors of landscapes hung on the walls. Twin beds had ornately carved wooden bedheads. The bathroom, which followed the angles of the octagonal tower, was marble-floored, with modern fittings. Like the bedroom, it was snugly heated.

The stone-flagged downstairs restaurant is arched; central wrought-iron lamps like medieval crowns are suspended above the tables, and antlers are mounted over the fireplace. A large family group was celebrating what seemed to be an engagement party, judging from the blushes of a self-conscious young couple. Much affectionately indulgent attention was also being lavished on a capricious octogenarian and a frisky, inquisitive toddler.

The food was very good, the service very correct; crumbs were swept carefully from the cloth with a silver pan and brush between courses, wine topped up, plates swiftly cleared. I opted for the selection of local hors d'oeuvres – almost always a good choice in paradors – which was served in the usual small brown glazed pottery dishes. Cheeses, asparagus, a morsel of pork in a red pepper sauce, eggs, a fish salad with vinaigrette dressing, jumbo shrimps, tiny olives, spicy sausages, and savory croquettes were among the tasty delicacies. I followed them with charcoal-roasted lamb flavored with rosemary and garlic, accompanied by smooth red Ribeiro wine. Galician pancakes, steeped in potent local liqueur, completed the meal.

I discovered a shop just round the corner that sold bread, olives, and cheese for my next day's picnic. I also bought some typical earthenware dishes, and enjoyed strolling about the town. When I asked whether the car would be safe, parked in front of the parador, the porter seemed surprised; the street crime which plagues the south does not yet seem to have touched this quiet corner of Galicia.

The massively thick fortress walls (opposite) shelter comfortable bedrooms. Above: the antler-decked cellar restaurant.

PARADOR NACIONAL CONDES DE VILLALBA, Valeriano Valdesuso, 27800 Villalba, Lugo. **Tel.** (82) 51 00 11. **Fax** (82) 51 00 90. **Owners** Spanish Government. **Open** All year. **Rooms** 6, all with bathroom (incl. wall shower), direct-dial phone, TV, minibar. **Facilities** Salon-bar, restaurant, elevator. **Restrictions** No dogs. **Terms** Moderate. **Credit cards** All major. **Closed parking** No. **Getting there** Madrid 545km via N VI. Turn off R at Baamonde; 17km to Villalba, parador signposted inside town. Int. airport, Santiago de Compostela, 110km. **Of local interest** Lugo (Roman town walls and cathedral). **Whole day expeditions** Ribadeo and parador; San Martin de Mondoñedo; picturesque countryside; scenic coastline. **Eating out** Ask at parador for small local eating places.

A royal hostelry

As a place of pilgrimage in the Middle Ages, the town of Santiago de Compostela ranked in importance with Jerusalem and Rome. Millions of people walked there from all over Europe, crossing mountain ranges and rivers to visit the shrine of St. James, and wearing in their hats the saint's scallop shell.

Getting there is easier today – you can fly into the international airport, or drive along the scenic but winding north coast road or up the busy highway from Madrid. On my first visit to Santiago I crossed the mountains by the pilgrim road, rich in Romanesque churches, pausing in O Cebreiro where the oval houses, thatched with heather, seem unchanged since the Stone Age.

Cabo Finisterre means "Cape at the World's End" – exactly what it was until the New World was discovered. In the countryside green fields alternate with oak and silver birch woodlands. Most farmhouses have an elaborate stone *horréo* or granary shaped like a tomb; trailing vines edge their fields. Much of Galicia's coastline has so far escaped the south's urbanization, and its *rías*, or inlets, have clear water and sandy beaches.

Santiago de Compostela is a friendly university city, the narrow streets of the oldest part of town crammed with small eating places. Flanking its vast main square are the soaring spires of the cathedral and the Hostal de los Reyes Católicos. Built in 1450 by Ferdinand and Isabella to lodge pilgrims, the Hostal's construction was overseen by the king and queen with great interest, so ensuring high-quality materials and craftsmanship. Its four courtyards are named for the four apostles.

Public rooms are majestic and tapestry hung; bedrooms are modern and snug. My room had recently been refurbished in deep blue brocade, tastefully patterned with tall purple irises. The marble-floored bathroom tiled in a restful cream was equipped with soft, fluffy white bath towels. The large main bedrooms overlooking the square have beds with velvet baldaquins, and adjoining sitting

rooms filled with antiques. As the main restaurant was being decorated during my visit, meals were being served in an arched undercroft. The food was excellent, the menu inviting, and the service polished, swift, and professional.

The cathedral is only a few steps away, magnificent and lofty. On great occasions it is perfumed by clouds of incense, as the immense silver censer, or *botafumeiro*, which hangs from the ceiling is swung to and fro. But the focal point for pilgrims is the small, peaceful room beneath the main altar where the silver casket said to contain the relics of St. James is displayed. During religious festivals – and during pop concerts held on the cathedral steps – the whole square fills up with people, so remember to check with the hotel as to which local events will be taking place during your visit if you want a quiet night's sleep.

Opposite and above: antiques grace a corridor and bedrooms. Overleaf: one of the arcaded courtyards which have welcomed pilgrims throughout the centuries.

HOSTAL DE LOS REYES CATÓLICOS, plaza de España 1, 15700 Santiago de Compostela. **Tel.** (81) 58 22 00. **Telex** 86004. **Fax** (81) 56 30 94. **Owners** Spanish Government. **Manager** Emilio Martín Manzanas. **Open** All year. **Rooms** 135, all with bathroom (incl. wall shower), direct-dial phone, TV, minibar. **Facilities** Salon, bar, restaurant, elevators, airconditioning, gardens, 4 conference rooms. **Restrictions** No dogs. **Terms** Expensive. **Credit cards** All major. **Closed parking** Yes, paying. **Getting there** Madrid 613km via N VI; int. airport 12km; follow signs to cathedral from edge of town. **Of local interest** Cathedral, old town. **Whole day expeditions** Coastal villages. **Eating out** Don Gaiferos, Anexo Vilas, La Tacita de Oro.

A nobleman's mansion

Granite-built beside a long inlet of the sea, Pontevedra has charming arcaded streets and squares with stone crosses. Legend has it that the town was founded by a Greek warrior who had fought at the siege of Troy, and for this reason it was formerly called "Helenes." The ancient part of the city can be explored on foot by stepping out of the parador gates into the little cobbled square that leads to narrow streets edged not only with historic churches and picturesque houses but also with many small, tempting *tapas* bars.

The Casa del Barón is a traditional Galician *pazo*, or manor house, a gracious aristocratic building designed for civilized living. Believed to stand on the site of a Roman villa, it was improved in both the 16th and 18th centuries, and was for many generations a family home. Early in the 19th century its owner died in battle; after that it served as a school, a public granary, a masonic lodge, and a rooming house until it passed once again into the hands of a noble family, who restored and lived in it. The Casa del Barón became a parador in 1955. Although it is in the city, it has a pleasant garden and, somewhat surprisingly, there is a further green lawn on a terrace one floor up.

You must arrive early to find a parking space inside the small courtyard, though cars left outside the gates should come to no harm. My arrival coincided with the end of a press conference held in the antique-filled sitting room of the parador, and I was amused to sit at lunch watching journalists checking their recordings of the gathering with pocket tape recorders pressed to their ears, while I sat in a corner muttering my impressions of them into mine. The dining room has glass-fronted vitrines displaying antique china. Brass chandeliers and sconces illuminate the room. There are wooden shutters and valances at the windows, gilt-framed mirrors and oil paintings on the walls. A flat arch and folding door divide the room in two. Pink carnations brightened the tables. I enjoyed my lunch among the noisy company. Freshly baked bread was served in a basket lined with a lace-edged cloth; local Galician vegetable soup with white beans, a lobster salad enlivened by green and red peppers in a vinaigrette, and a feather-light almond tart were all good, and pleasantly and briskly served.

My bedroom, which had simple carved wooden bedheads, leather armchairs, and a polished wood floor, looked out over the garden. Most rooms are small, so if you want space request a suite or the 3-bed large family room. There are quiet extra sitting areas in the wide corridors upstairs. Rooms in a new wing are virtually identical to the original ones.

The granite walls of the entry hall glint with tiny silvery flecks. Note above the door the statue of a saint, who, I was told, is the Spanish equivalent of Rip Van Winkle, portrayed with a little bird perched on his shoulder. You will enjoy exploring Pontevedra – be sure to see the prehistoric treasures of its Museo Provincial.

Opposite: the cool, antique-filled salon and the bougainvillea-clad façade. Above: roses from the parador's garden.

PARADOR NACIONAL CASA DEL BARÓN, plaza de Maceda, 36002 Pontevedra. **Tel.** (86) 85 58 00. **Fax** (86) 85 21 95. **Owners** Spanish Government. **Manager** José Basso Puga. **Open** All year. **Rooms** 47, all with bathroom (incl. wall shower), direct-dial phone, TV, minibar. **Facilities** Salon, bar, restaurant, elevator, garden, 2 conference rooms. **Restrictions** No dogs in restaurant. **Terms** Moderate. **Credit cards** All major. **Closed parking** 12 car spaces in courtyard, free. **Getting there** Madrid 599km via Orense, Verín, Benavente. Circle town to enter from S. along river, parador signposted in old town. **Of local interest** Explore coastline to Cambados (parador), beaches and villages. **Whole day expeditions** Santiago de Compostela (see p. 31), Bayona (see p. 41). **Eating out** Casa Solla, Doña Antonia, Casa Román.

Twenties nostalgia

How many hotels in the world are there where you can look out of your bedroom window and see the chef selecting the day's fish from a fishing boat tied up at the hotel jetty?

The Gran Hotel on the island of La Toja has tremendous nostalgic charm. It stands among palm-tree-lined avenues and pine groves, overlooking a clear, turquoise-blue sea. Built in 1907, it has the spaciousness and style of another era, with its wide terraces, marble-floored ballroom, white wicker chairs under bright yellow awnings, original stained glass, casino, spa, and wedding chapel. Linking it to the mainland is an ornate, cast-iron bridge. You half expect to come across Somerset Maugham in a panama hat dozing by the pool. This site was chosen for a hotel because of the famed curative properties of its mineral spring, as well as for its glorious setting.

Few guests arrive today as formerly, with an entourage of valets, personal maids, chauffeurs, and secretaries, though European royalty and Rockefellers have always spent family holidays here, and, like the heads of state and industry who arrive for conferences, appreciate the three helipads and the security advantages of an island site. For newsworthy gatherings, a press office is rapidly installed with up to fifty direct phone lines.

Most of the staff have been here for years – new recruits attend the in-house hotel school before being allowed to serve guests, who are always addressed by their names. Grandchildren of original guests are frequent visitors.

At tea-time, you can order Earl Grey or Lapsang Souchong, Darjeeling or Orange Pekoe, or even the Prince of Wales's special blend; you will find the barman mixes an expert White Lady or a Gin Fizz.

The extensive grounds, beaches and tennis courts, play areas and swings, make the Gran Hotel ideal for family holidays, though the children I saw were so beautifully behaved that they never inconvenienced other guests. Rates are lower in winter, but flowers

still bloom and oranges still hang on the trees. Bedrooms have been refurbished with floral chintz and new mattresses to fit the original brass bedsteads; they have kept their mahogany furniture. The tiled bathrooms are being modernized. Most of the bedrooms are moderately sized, though the royal suite has a wide terrace, two bedrooms, and a sitting room. Be sure to ask for a room with a view.

You may have wondered, now that high-rise hotels have blighted the Costas, where the Spanish themselves get away from it all to spend their summer holidays. The answer is, here in Galicia. Although new hotels and villas are being built, much of the coastline remains unspoilt. The clean, golden-sand beaches make this a perfect spot for small children, while the pretty wooded countryside inland and the mountains on the borders of the province make it ideal for touring. Galicia is one of Spain's best kept secrets.

Palms fill the immaculately kept gardens (opposite above) and can be glimpsed from the terrace at tea-time (opposite below). Above: a mirror reflects a brass bedstead and chintz. Overleaf: dawn breaks by the pool, overlooking the sea.

GRAN HOTEL DE LA TOJA, 36991 Isla de la Toja, Pontevedra. **Tel.** (86) 73 00 25. **Telex** 88042. **Fax** (86) 73 12 01. **Owners** La Toja S.A. **Manager** Antonio Franco Cantos. **Open** All year. **Rooms** 198, all with bathroom (incl. wall shower), direct-dial phone, satellite TV, radio, room service (no minibars), laundry. **Facilities** Salon, bar, restaurant, elevators, pool with buffet, gardens, 4 reception/conference rooms, chapel, casino, health and beauty spa. Beach, 9-hole golf, tennis. Sailing/wind-surfing/shooting/fishing/hunt- ing/riding by arrangement. **Restrictions** No dogs. **Terms** Expensive/deluxe. **Credit cards** All major. **Closed parking** Yes, free. **Getting there** Madrid 637km via N VI to Santiago, motorway to Pontevedra 33km away. Int. airport at Santiago, helicopter by arrangement. **Of local interest** Coastline and inlets. **Whole day expeditions** Santiago de Compostela (see p. 31); Bayona (see p. 41). **Eating out** El Crisol, La Dorna, Posada des Mar, El Pirata.

Gateway to the New World

My room in the Parador de Turismo Conde de Gondomar looked out over the Vigo bay, into which the small galleon *Pinta* sailed when it brought back the first news of Columbus's discovery of the New World. Islands – the Islas Cias – fringed with sandy beaches mark the entrance to the bay. At night I fell asleep to the sound of the sea beating fiercely on the rocks below. I woke to find the palest of blue seas only faintly rippled by the long V-shaped wake of a fishing boat leaving harbor.

Earlier versions of this castle of Monterreal were held by the Carthaginians in the 2nd century BC against the invading Romans, and were later successfully defended against Sir Francis Drake, under the leadership of the 18-year-old count for whom the parador is named. He became ambassador to the English court of James I. The castle has been rebuilt and its enclosing walls repaired. Walking around the complete circuit is about 3 kilometers, a pleasant early-morning stroll for the athletic.

Rooms with a sea view are a fair distance from the entrance. Other rooms look into an inner court and gardens. There are some elaborate suites with four-poster beds and sitting rooms, but my room was simple: lozenge-shaped red tiles on the floor, sturdy wooden furniture, pleasant prints on the walls, and a good modern bathroom with separate shower stall.

The people of Galicia have their own language, fulls of xs, and their province has much of the same atmosphere and unspoilt charm as parts of Brittany and Ireland, whose peoples share the same Celtic ancestry, legends, granite coast, and bagpipes.

This is a place to enjoy seafood. In a tank in the restaurant, which overlooks the gardens, gigantic lobsters and crabs await their fate. Decorative wine barrels, yokes for oxen, and earthenware pitchers add interest to the room. I enjoyed the hot and cold hors d'oeuvres: fifteen separate tiny earthenware dishes, including a demi-tasse of rich crab soup, mussels with a delicious stuffing, large juicy shrimp, pieces of fresh tuna in a tasty vinaigrette, spicy sausage in a bun, a

slice of broccoli quiche, smoked ham with pineapple, smoked salmon, potato croquettes, and hot fish in a savory tomato sauce. My main course was a splendidly succulent lobster salad and I rounded off the meal with a smooth papaya sorbet.

Local white Ribeiro wine is good, and resembles nearby Portugal's *vinho verde*, or green wine. (The green refers to its fresh taste, not its color; it can also be red.) As well as expensive vintage wines, the paradors serve reasonably priced local wine which always goes well with local dishes, and which surprised me with its smoothness.

I found the parador comfortable, its food more than worthy of the high culinary reputation of the province, and this promontory, overlooking the yacht club and islands, a most enchanting place to spend a relaxed and peaceful holiday.

This parador is noted for its fine seafood (opposite). Its historic past lives on in the cannon which still guard it (above), and (overleaf) in the armor worn by its knights and the encircling walls which can be seen from the restaurant.

PARADOR DE TURISMO CONDE DE GONDOMAR, ctra de Bayona, 36300 Pontevedra. **Tel.** (86) 35 50 00. **Telex** 83424. **Fax** (86) 35 50 76. **Owners** Spanish Government. **Manager** Rafael Vazquez. **Open** All year. **Rooms** 124, all with bathroom (incl. wall shower), direct-dial phone, 7-channel TV, radio; 40 with minibar. **Facilities** Salon, bar, restaurant, pool, gardens, 5 conference rooms. NB No elevator. **Terms** Expensive. **Credit cards** All major. **Restrictions** No dogs. **Closed parking** Yes, paying. **Getting there** Madrid 616km via N VI, Benavente, Orense, Vigo. Approaching Bayona, drive to far end of town, where castle is visible. **Of local interest** Monastery of Santa María de Oya 15km; Túy 21km. **Whole day expeditions** Into Portugal; Pontevedra (see p. 35); Santiago de Compostela (see p. 31). **Eating out** Small local restaurants Moscón, Rocamar, Pedro Madruga, Tunel, Bayona, etc.

Within famous city walls

Standing impressively against a backdrop of the snow-capped Gredos mountains, Avila is the highest town in Spain. Some 3700 feet above sea level, it crowns uplands strewn with boulders fretted into strange shapes by the wind, and dotted with the deserted forts of Stone Age man. Perhaps this too was a Stone Age site – certainly the Celts lived here, leaving behind their curiously carved statues of boars and bulls.

The walls that enclose the city are its great glory – probably the finest in Spain. Nine imposing gates defend access to the city, and eighty-eight towers – one formed by the apse of the cathedral – strengthen the walls which are 40 feet high and 10 feet thick. Completed in 1099, they are built on the original Roman foundations, using stones from Celtic, Roman, and Arab fortifications, or anything else that came to hand – you can spot inscriptions and carvings on some which were once tombstones or monuments.

The work was supervised by King Alfonso VI's son-in-law, Count Raymond of Burgundy, who had just defeated the Moors (and after whom the parador is named). The city was repopulated by noblemen and their followers from all over Spain, earning Avila the title "Avila de los Caballeros" ("Knightly Avila"). St. Teresa of Avila, the great mystic and reformer of the Carmelite order, was born here in 1515.

The road to the town climbs steadily upward, the groves of trees and wandering herds of cows with their guardian and his dog a relief after the flat monotony of the plains. On approaching Avila take the signs to the "Ciudad Vieja" ("Old Town"); follow the walls round to the right and enter through the Carmen gate, which is signposted to the parador.

A copy of a Celtic bull stands in the parador's courtyard, which is shaded by an immense pine tree taller than the roof. Tiled and arched arcades surround it – a reminder of the city's Arab past. A suit of armor guards the entrance. Ask for a room facing the garden, and looking towards the walls and towards the storks' nest by the gateway. I liked the simplicity of the rooms: wrought-iron lamps and crucifix, handwoven bedcovers with a bird motif, polished wooden floor, and white-tiled bathroom. The parador staff were helpful, the welcome warm, and the local specialty, *judias del barco de Avila* (a bean stew with chorizo sausages), hearty and full of flavor. The house wine is an excellent Marqués de Cáceres Rioja, or try Marqués de Riscal from Rueda – a town you pass through if you come here from León. *Tapas* are served at the bar, and the breakfast buffet was heaped with good things.

You must not leave the area without seeing nearby Segovia. If you wish to spend more than a day there you can stay in the modern parador just outside the city. Visit its Romanesque churches, amazing Roman aqueduct, and ornate Alcázar. Both Avila and Segovia have fine cathedrals and fascinating streets to explore; they present a complete contrast in atmosphere and appearance, and neither should be missed.

Opposite: standing in a garden tucked inside city walls, this parador offers guests views of nesting storks and a tranquil, shaded courtyard. Above: four-posters in a peaceful bedroom.

PARADOR NACIONAL RAIMUNDO DE BORGOÑA, Marqués de Canales y Chozas 16, 05001 Avila. **Tel.** (18) 21 13 40. **Fax** (18) 22 61 66. **Owners** Spanish Government. **Manager** Alejandro Piñuela Otero. **Open** All year. **Rooms** 62, all with bathroom (incl. wall shower), direct-dial phone, TV, minibar. **Facilities** Salon, bar, restaurant with airconditioning, elevator, garden, 2 conference rooms. **Restrictions** No dogs. **Terms** Moderate. **Credit cards** All major. **Closed parking** Yes, paying. **Getting there** Madrid 107km, via N VI motorway, exit 4. Parador signposted in Avila. **Of local interest** Climb town walls near parador; churches of S. Vicente, S. Pedro, S. Segundo; provincial museum; Puerta de Alcázar; Plaza Sta Teresa; cathedral; Los Toros de Guisando, Las Cogotas, Celtic monuments. **Whole day expeditions** Arévalo (17th-century town); Arenas de San Pedro castle; Sierra de Gredos parador and mountains, nature reserve, Guisando and Mombeltrán villages; Segovia (Roman aqueduct, Romanesque churches, cathedral, Alcázar, parador). **Eating out** Small restaurants Capacabana, Mesón El Sol, El Rastro.

Sophisticated luxury

The Ritz Madrid is Spain's most prestigious hotel. It stands facing the three elaborate fountains that adorn the Paseo del Prado, in the heart of the capital. The Prado itself, one of the world's major art collections, is just across the road. Like London's Claridges, the Ritz Madrid is used by royalty as a sort of annex to the palace, and by the aristocracy as a home from home. The manager seemed somewhat distracted when I interviewed him before leaving, no doubt because the King of Spain was lunching at the hotel the same day.

The fact that the hotel exists at all is largely thanks to another king, Alfonso XIII; when in 1906 he married Victoria Eugenia, granddaughter of England's Queen Victoria, he realized that there was no suitable establishment in Madrid to accommodate royal guests. At his instigation, César Ritz created this hotel, which was completed in 1910.

You register at the reception desk in the lofty circular entrance hall. Drinks are served in the Lower Hall, and afternoon tea in the Upper Hall – enormous rooms with ornate plasterwork and gorgeous flower decorations – to the accompaniment of gentle piano-playing. There is no bar as such, but you can sit on white wicker chairs under blue and white parasols in the elegant leafy terrace gardens during the day, enjoying breakfast, a cup of coffee, a cool drink, or a light snack. At night floodlights brighten the gardens and the gleaming façade of the hotel.

People eat fashionably late in Madrid. Having flown in and spent an exhausting day tramping round the Prado, I was the first guest to enter the restaurant, when others were only just beginning to gather for a pre-dinner drink. I was welcomed warmly, pampered by regiments of liveried staff in this glorious turn-of-the-century, tapestried room, and entertained by a gentleman harpist with a selection of Fifties tunes.

My table was lit by a tall, branched, silver candlestick, ringed round the base with a circlet of orange and yellow flowers. It is always a delight when the caliber of the food in a restaurant matches the opulence of the decor, and here it did: smoked duck-breast salad beautifully presented, meltingly succulent calf's liver with tiny tender green beans, a feather-light raspberry mousse, exquisite petits fours with my coffee. Breakfast, served on Wedgwood china, was equally memorable.

The bedroom had an enormous walk-in closet; a large silver tray of fruit awaited me. The hotel's unique period carpets are thick and elaborately patterned – here in golden leafy swirls. The gray-marble bathroom was as large as the bedroom, with a robe, a fresh yellow rose, and generous toiletries. The linen sheets were turned back while I dined, my nightdress neatly laid out. Maids in black dresses and crisp white aprons greeted me politely when we met in corridors.

Trusthouse Forte now own the Ritz Madrid, and they are maintaining its tradition of splendor and expensive exclusiveness.

Opposite: regal sophistication in the lofty entrance hall, with its magnificent sweeping staircase, and in the ornate Upper Hall. Above: a luxurious bathroom. Overleaf: the gorgeous turn-of-the-century restaurant.

HOTEL RITZ, plaza de la Lealtad 5, 28014 Madrid. **Tel.** (1) 521 28 57. **Telex** 43986. **Fax** (1) 532 87 76. **Owners** Trusthouse Forte Int. Hotels. **Manager** John M. Macedo. **Open** All year. **Rooms** 156 (incl. 26 suites), all with bathroom (incl. wall shower), direct-dial phone, satellite TV, minibar, airconditioning, room service, laundry/dry cleaning/ironing. **Facilities** Salon, restaurant, garden restaurant, barber shop and beauty salon, safe deposit boxes, 6 conference rooms. Audio-visual/bilingual secretarial service/simultaneous translation/private fax machine/limousine/private helicopter/baby sitting/private stalking, shooting/private guided tours of Prado etc. by arrangement. **Restrictions** Dogs by arrangement only. **Terms** Super-deluxe. Ask about gourmet dinners, all-inclusive weekends, Christmas and New Year menus. **Credit cards** All major. **Closed parking** Yes, paying. **Getting there** Airport 13km. **Of local interest** Prado, Retiro park, Archaeological Museum, Goya Pantheon, etc. Ask at hotel. **Whole day expeditions** Avila and Segovia (see p. 45); Chinchón and Aranjuez (see p. 53); El Escorial; Alcalá de Henares; Toledo (see p. 73). **Eating out** Fortuny, Zalacaín, Jockey.

Stylish elegance

I arrived at the Palace Hotel in Madrid to discover that my travel agent had booked me in for the wrong day. Given that I was there secretly to inspect the hotel, this was highly frustrating. It was also a good test of staff attitudes. I am happy to say that I received sympathy, concern, and help, and a room was found for me without my having to reveal my mission.

The moment you enter the Palace Hotel you sense its great personality. A gracious, stylish building, situated between the Parliament and the Prado, it has always played host to eminent politicians, visiting statesmen, and the world's leading figures in the arts. Mata Hari, Ernest Hemingway, Artur Rubinstein, and François Mitterand have all stayed here. It does not dwell on its past glories, however, but concentrates on ensuring that its present guests have every modern comfort. The hotel feels alive, welcoming, and efficient, sure signs that it has a good manager. The spacious entrance hall is lined with amply staffed reception and concierge desks, so checking in or out is brisk, and enquiries promptly answered; luggage arrives immediately in the room.

In the public rooms the seemingly infinite number of agreeable sitting areas – under the wonderful glass dome and its feathery glass chandeliers, in the elegantly intimate bar, or tucked into alcoves in the central rotunda – make this a perfect place for meeting friends or talking business, and a favorite haunt of members of Parliament. Hotel guests also appreciate the convenience of the newsstand, boutique with a tempting selection of high-quality goods, travel agent, barber shop, and beauty salon. A shopping arcade, the "Galería del Prado," with thirty-nine shops, and "La Plaza," a coffee shop/restaurant, have also been recently opened beneath the hotel.

The menu in the main restaurant is light, well balanced, and appetizing, ranging from caviar, oysters, and local specialties to grills, fish, and enticing desserts. The coffee shop, "El Ambigu," offers weekend buffets with crisp, fresh salads and cold salmon, crayfish, cold cuts, and fruit dishes. Table service here is courteous and attentive and "El Ambigu" is open from 11.30am to 2.30am.

I was pleased to find a telephone on the desk as well as beside the bed in my spacious room, with its deep blue brocade bedcover, matching armchair and drapes, fitted carpet, and luxurious bathroom. Before leaving I was able to inspect a range of magnificent suites, with large and elegantly furnished sitting rooms, lavishly comfortable bedrooms, glamorous bathrooms, long ranges of closets, and an extra bathroom for guests. I was impressed by the choice of evening entertainment offered to conventions. Classical ballet, Spanish dancing, fashion shows, and cookery demonstrations, all of which are arranged in-house, are part of an enterprising and imaginative selection.

The Palace Hotel combines the charm of a historic setting with the advantages of an efficient, up-to-date, modern hotel.

The famous and the fashionable meet under the splendid glass dome (opposite). Above: one of the lavishly appointed bedrooms.

PALACE HOTEL, plaza de las Cortes 7, 28014 Madrid. **Tel.** (1) 429 75 51. **Telex** 23903; 22272 (reservations). **Fax** (1) 429 82 66. **Owners** International Hotels Corporation. **Director** Juan José Bergés. **Open** All year. **Rooms** 500 (incl. 29 suites), all with bathroom (incl. wall shower), direct-dial phone, satellite TV, optional video, 100 with radio, minibar, airconditioning. Laundry/dry cleaning/ironing service except Sun. **Facilities** Salon, 2 bars, 3 restaurants, 4 elevators, airconditioning, newsstand, boutique, beauty and barber shop, travel agent, large shopping center, 9 conference rooms. Audio-visual/secretarial/simultaneous translation/limousine services. Dictaphone/typewriter/ portable fax/printer for personal computer/video recorder available. **Restrictions** No dogs in public rooms. **Terms** Super-deluxe. **Credit cards** All major. **Closed parking** Yes, paying. **Getting there** Follow signs for Prado. Airport 13km. **Of local interest** Prado, Archaeological Museum, Goya Pantheon, etc. Ask at hotel about antique and other shopping. **Whole day expeditions** Avila and Segovia (see p. 45); La Granja; El Escorial; Toledo (see p. 73); Aranjuez and Chinchón (see p. 53); Riaza; Atienza; Sigüenza; Pedraza de la Sierra. **Eating out** Zalacaín, El Cenador del Prado, Lúculo, Fortuny, Príncipe de Viana.

Excellent cuisine and monastery gardens

I cannot imagine a lovelier setting for a hotel than this parador in Chinchón. Tree-shaded and peaceful, the cloisters of this former Augustinian monastery enclose cool, trickling fountains and a terraced garden fragrant with roses, pomegranate trees, and orange blossom. White fantailed pigeons coo on the roof. In quiet corners green-baize tables are set out for card playing; the bar is bright with ornamental blue tiles and copper. One staircase has its original murals, and in the plate-glass-enclosed cloisters are more recent modern murals and striking tapestries, both depicting saints.

At the weekend the entire place hums with activity as fashionably elegant Madrileños drive up for lunch, and families gather complete with their oldest and youngest members to celebrate an engagement or birthday. The road from Madrid passes the palace and gardens at Aranjuez, leads through long straight leafy avenues, past fields and olive groves, climbing to the small, balcony-lined village square of Chinchón which doubles as a bullring.

It was a countess of Chinchón, wife of Spain's viceroy to Peru in the 17th century, who after having been cured of a fever by an infusion of tree bark brought the remedy back to Europe, where it was called *chinchona* in her honor. Today we know it as quinine.

Note the fine chapel on the left of the monastery's massive main door. Bedrooms are charming, with 3-foot-thick, color-washed walls, flower-painted wooden furniture, and shutters. The tiled floors are spread with patterned Spanish rugs. A delightful linen hanging embroidered with fantastical bright flowers decorated one wall of my room. There were comfortable green velvet armchairs, a desk, and by the bedside a converted oil-lamp with a tall chimney. The tiled modern bathroom was extremely well-equipped.

Before dinner I sat in the bar and sampled the powerful local aniseed drink, served with water, which tasted something like arak. The food was the best I had eaten in any parador, stylishly presented and served on Villeroy and Bosch china. I chose game soup, capped with a puff-pastry lid, roast venison flavored with juniper, duchesse potatoes, spicy red cabbage, puréed chestnuts, and a rich red wine sauce. The light fresh fig mousse for dessert was served with a mango coulis. It was an exceptionally fine meal, in which all the details – the fresh crunchy bread, well-ironed napkins, unsalted creamy butter – were perfect. I can well understand why people from Madrid take the trouble and time to drive up here to eat.

I enjoyed my stay in all the paradors I visited, and would commend them to any visitor to Spain, but this enchanting monastery at Chinchón is probably my favorite.

Situated in flower-filled terraced gardens (opposite), this former monastery provides the varied delights of a tiled bar (above), and (overleaf) a courtyard fragrant with roses, a stairway with its original murals, and charmingly simple bedrooms.

PARADOR NACIONAL DE CHINCHÓN, Generalissimo 1, 28370 Chinchón, Madrid. **Tel.** (1) 894 08 36. **Telex** 49398. **Fax** (1) 894 09 08. **Owners** Spanish Government. **Manager** D. Antonio Bertolín Blasco. **Open** All year. **Rooms** 38, all with bathroom (incl. wall shower), direct-dial phone, TV, radio, minibar. **Facilities** Salon, bar, restaurant, airconditioning, pool, gardens, 4 conference rooms. NB No elevator.

Restrictions No dogs. **Terms** Moderate. **Closed parking** Yes, paying. **Getting there** Madrid 52km, turning off N IV. **Of local interest** Local churches (one said to have an altarpiece by Goya), Aranjuez palace and gardens. **Whole day expeditions** Alcalá de Henares; Toledo (see p. 73); Madrid (see pp. 47, 51). **Eating out** Small local restaurants, ask at parador.

Culinary delights high in the Pyrenees

Snow was still lying on the Pyrenees when I drove up via a good but winding road from Perpignan toward Andorra in late April. I briefly found myself above the snowline, before dropping down to the gentle plain on which Seo de Urgel stands, ringed by majestic mountains.

This is a summer resort area with many hotels and a constant stream of bargain seekers en-route to duty-free Andorra, quieter early or late in the year. I inspected the Hotel Boix on the French side of Seo de Urgel at Martinet, a restaurant-with-rooms backing on to a river, with spacious, close-carpeted or wooden-floored bedrooms, and serving excellent food. Its all-in pension price looked good value. I saw also the luxurious parador in the town center, which has a spectacular inner covered courtyard with hanging plants, an indoor pool, attractive bedrooms, and marble-floored corridors. Either of these I thought would be enjoyable.

It was, however, the view and the mouthwatering meal which finally made me decide on El Castell. The ruined 12th-century Castillo de Terreblanca stands on a commanding height beyond the town, and is used by the hotel owners as a private enclosure in which vegetables are grown and chickens raised for the restaurant.

The actual hotel building is in fact modern, with fairly small motel-type rooms each with its own balcony – you could find yourself cramped if you took half-a-dozen large bags into the room with you. But breakfast on the terrace in the morning as you look at the mountains, the river below, and the house-martins darting about between the pine trees in the sloping terraced rose garden, more than compensates.

A dip in the hotel pool is reviving; and so, after sightseeing in town, is a perfectly served lunch – request a table beside the huge plate-glass windows.

The creamy crab bisque, trout from a local river with wild mushroom stuffing, and chocolate mille-feuille were all delectable. The table was set with a silver bowl filled with fragrant pink roses from the hotel's own garden.

The rooms are furnished with dark wood fittings and shiny satin bedcovers. They are well-equipped, with satellite TV, modern bathroom, and a desk incorporating a comprehensive minibar. The hotel has one small sitting room, with a view, and a further spacious sitting room and bar at the back, without a view.

The owners' son has studied at hotel school and has worked in some of Europe's best hotels, which like El Castell are members of the prestigious Relais et Chateaux organization. He will shortly be returning to help his parents open a second hotel, and to continue developing the castle itself, which the family has been working hard to maintain and improve. They hope one day to open the castle and its gardens to visitors to this beautiful corner of the Pyrenees.

Breakfast on the terrace (above) overlooks the panoramic mountain view shown opposite.

HOTEL EL CASTELL, 25700 Seo de Urgel, Lérida. **Tel.** (73) 35 07 04; 35 10 41. **Telex** 93610. **Fax** (73) 35 15 74. **Owner/ Manager** Jaume Tapies Travé. **Open** All year except 15 Jan.–15 Feb. **Rooms** 40, all with bathroom (incl. wall shower), direct-dial phone, TV, music channel, minibar, some with airconditioning, safe. **Facilities** 2 salons, bar, 2 restaurants, pool, gardens, 2 conference rooms. Skiing, golf 40km, tennis 2km. **Restrictions** No dogs in restaurant.

Terms Deluxe. **Credit cards** All major. **Closed parking** Yes, free. **Getting there** Madrid 602km via N II, Zaragoza and Lérida. **Of local interest** Seo de Urgel (medieval streets, cathedral, local twice-weekly market, parador), Andorra. **Whole day expeditions** Solsona; Barcelona. **Eating out** Mesón Teo, La Borda de l'Avi, La Taberna dels Noguers, Hotel Boix, La Borda, El Xopluc.

A gourmet hideaway

I must admit to a weakness for tiny, highly idiosyncratic hotels lost in the countryside, especially if their food is wonderful. Mas Pau is a beamed 16th-century Catalan farmhouse, smothered in creeper, standing among fields at the end of a long track. It is a few kilometers outside Figueras, 20 kilometers from the French border. The Catalans have a strong feeling of identity, use their own language and spelling of place names, and are proud of their native sons, Pau Casals and Salvador Dalí. Foreigners receive a friendly welcome.

After parking on the gravel forecourt, I walked through the gardens, admiring the big earthenware pots, massed flowers, ancient millstone, and tempting pool. Once inside I found myself in a low-ceilinged bar which had the air of an antique shop, crammed with tables made from old treadle sewing machines, wicker chairs, tin candlesticks, carved couches, embroidered cushions, pub mirrors, and a period piano. A thick plate-glass door reveals the bottles in the cellar beyond.

Note, if steps are a problem, that the restaurant is upstairs. Its brightly polished wooden floor gleams beneath sloping beams from which hangs an assortment of ornate painted and gilded oil lamps converted to electricity. Portraits of stout ladies and assertive-looking gentlemen, rural landscapes, and flower paintings cover the stone walls, and on every table and ledge stand great vasefuls of white and purple lilac. I ordered pea soup, vividly green with a bright red crayfish in the middle of the bowl, tender duck with a caramelized sauce, accompanied by tiny fresh figs previously soaked in brandy, and an oven-baked potato which had been scooped out, deliciously seasoned, and replaced in the skin. There is an impressive wine list, including the best vintages of the finest French wines, as well as Spanish. A chilled dry white Penedés and a full-bodied red Montilla complemented the meal to perfection. When I asked if I might have strawberries with my fresh meringue,

they were whisked away, hulled, sliced, and beautifully arranged. Other desserts looked equally tempting, and even the petits fours with the coffee were special – mini-madeleines, wafer thin bitter chocolate tiles, and freshly made truffles wrapped round cointreau-dipped candied orange. Not surprisingly, the restaurant is Michelin-starred and well patronized.

There are seven spacious motel-style bedrooms beside the forecourt, which are completely modern apart from heavy wooden shutters. Each has a sitting area with couch, easy chairs, a glass-topped coffee table, and a handy minibar, divided from the bedroom area by a range of hanging closets. The bedroom area has a king-sized bed, good reading lights, and a stand for clothes. The luxury marble bathroom has a powerful shower. As one might imagine, breakfast served on German china ornamented with pink wild roses was lavish: croissants, Danish pastries, four kinds of home-made preserves, and honey tasting of wild flowers.

No wonder that French guests often cross the border for a meal and a comfortable night's stay. Any gourmet will find Mas Pau well worth the journey.

Opposite: the beamed, Michelin-starred restaurant shelters under the creeper-clad, tiled roof of this 16th-century farmhouse. Above: lobster, the specialty of the house.

RESTAURANT-HOTEL MAS PAU, carretera de Olot, 17742 Figueras, Girona. **Tel.** (72) 54 61 54. **Fax** (72) 50 13 77. **Owners** Restaurant Mas Pau S.A. **Manager** Nuria Serrat Bofill. **Open** All year except 2nd Wed. in Jan–1st Fri. in March. **Rooms** 7, all with bathroom (incl. wall shower), direct-dial phone, satellite TV, minibar, airconditioning. **Facilities** Salon, bar, restaurant, pool, gardens, 3 private dining/conference rooms for 15/40/200 people. **Restrictions** None. **Terms** Expensive. **Credit cards** All major.

Closed parking Forecourt gate shut at night. **Getting there** Madrid 744km via N II motorway to Barcelona, Girona, France. Turn off at Figueras, in town take Olot road; after 5km hotel on L at Avinyonet de Puigventós. **Of local interest** Figueras Dalí museum, Sant Pere de Roda (Romanesque church), Besalú. **Whole day expeditions** Barcelona 135km by motorway; modern parador at Vich in mountains. **Eating out** See Mas de Torrent (p. 61).

Country chic

In Catalonia, the word *mas* means "farmhouse," just as it does in Provence. The Mas de Torrent, on the edge of the ancient hamlet of Torrent not far from the coast, is a handsome sandstone farm which has been transformed with style and taste into one of Spain's most delightful hotels. Woven rush mats in the hall, four huge earthenware pots for the tall rubber trees in the entrance porch, pine country antiques, and great armfuls of vivid poppies and cornflowers complement the massively thick color-washed walls, charming fabrics, and modern prints. The sprawling building has many different sitting areas: by the hearth in the long comfortable salon, in the quiet card room, tucked into a corner of the small bar, and upstairs in the wide upper hall whose floor-to-ceiling window faces the gardens. There is even an anteroom to the restaurant with invitingly deep sofas where one can study the menu over a glass of sherry before eating under the high timber roof, looking out over a panoramic vista of flowers, olive and palm trees, and misty blue hills. Both food and service are outstanding. There are terraces and pergolas in sun and in shade, and sunbeds on which to relax beside the pool.

Elegant Barcelona residents mix happily with honeymooning couples and family groups – this is also a favorite hideaway for small, select, exclusive seminars, and the bronzed and relaxed top international management of a famous Dutch electronics firm were just leaving with loud regrets as I arrived.

Each of the bedrooms in the main building, which dates from 1751, has its own character – some retain the original ornate plasterwork ceilings. They vary in size but all have been carefully furnished with delightful antiques, and have luxurious modern bathrooms cleverly and unobtrusively incorporated. Even the doors to the rooms are ancient, clearly showing the marks of the hand adze used to trim their boards. There are only eight of these specially attractive rooms so book well in advance to secure one, though further rooms added under terracotta tiled roofs a few steps from the main door and pool are extremely comfortable and spacious. Mine, with its cool decor of white, vivid blue, and pale yellow, had square wicker easy chairs and sofa, a coffee table stacked with glossy magazines, wicker bedhead, extensive closet space, efficient airconditioning, and a marble bathroom. Double-glazed doors open on to a sun terrace, facing a wheatfield.

There is a sophisticated menu with dishes which taste as good as they sound. Everything was excellent: a delicious red mullet cooked to perfection "en papillote"; a crisp mixed salad which I was able to select from a trolley brought to the table and served to my choice, with a selection of dressings; and chocolate mousse with a minty sauce, rich but not heavy. Service was highly professional yet friendly, and I prophesy that this comparatively recently opened hotel, which has all the polish of a town establishment combined with the charm of a rural location and decor, will become an obligatory stop-over for discriminating international travelers.

Imaginative decor (above) is a feature of this ancient farmhouse. The cool, arched entrance hall (opposite) contrasts with the sun-drenched gardens. Overleaf: a snug corner of the bar; the tempting pool is overlooked by some of the balconied bedrooms.

HOTEL MAS DE TORRENT, 17123 Torrent, Girona. **Tel.** (72) 30 32 92. **Telex** 56398. **Fax** (72) 30 32 93. **Owner** D. Juan Figueras. **Managers** Family Figueras. **Open** All year. **Rooms** 30, all with bathroom (incl. wall shower), direct-dial phone, TV, radio, minibar, airconditioning, safe. **Facilities** Salon, bar, restaurant, airconditioning, pool, gardens, 3 conference rooms, tennis. NB No elevator, but many ground-floor rooms. **Restrictions** Dogs in some rooms only. **Terms** Deluxe. **Credit cards** All major. **Closed parking** Yes, free. **Getting there** Madrid 744km via N II, then motorway Zaragoza, Lérida, Barcelona, Girona. **Of local interest** Medieval towns of Torrent, Pals, Peratallada; ceramics in La Bisbal. **Whole day expeditions** Bagur, coast; Sa Tuna, Aigua Blava (modern parador on cliff-top); Aiguafreda; Barcelona (see p. 69). **Eating out** Big Rock (Playa de Aro), Sa Punta (Pals), Hotel Ampurdán (Figueras).

Seaside grandeur

Eating a delicious breakfast on the terrace of my room at La Gavina (The Seagull) was one of the pleasantest experiences of my time in Spain. It was late April, the weather was perfect, the sun glinting on the sea. I watched a sleek white pleasure boat leave for a day's fishing. A scent of pine floated towards me from the forest of trees thickly covering the peninsula, vividly green against the red earth.

I was glad to be in a room on this side of the hotel, facing out to sea – rooms at the front are larger and grander, but face the relentlessly encroaching tide of buildings across the bay. The upper floors are simply furnished in chintzes, somehow more appropriate to a seaside setting than the rich velvet, brocade paneling, and chandeliers of the suites – though not perhaps if one had arrived in the ancient Bentley which was parked by the front door as I drove up. I was delighted to discover that the original giant shower heads had been retained in the modernized, well-equipped bathrooms. My room was spacious, and the closets enormous.

I spent an enjoyable day further up the coast, exploring the unspoilt coves and minute fishing villages hidden at the foot of roads which drop steeply down in a series of hairpin bends between villas half-hidden in the trees. The modern parador at Aigua-blava is perched on cliffs above startlingly turquoise water. Inland, many of the medieval villages seem so far unspoilt by tourism, and April is a glorious month for the wildflowers that run riot over roadsides and fields. Like the Mistral in Provence, the Tramontana wind can be bothersome, but it was not blowing during my visit.

La Gavina is a stately Thirties hotel with gardens and smooth green lawns. Its poolside terrace restaurant is shaded by pine trees. Inside, beyond the mosaic-floored entrance hall, lie a series of richly decorated restaurants, a bar like the cabin of a sailing ship, a salon warmed by an open fire, and a card room reminiscent of a London gentlemen's club.

Happily, however, it has moved with the times. Computers ensure efficiency; conference rooms are fully equipped with audio-visual technology; and a recent change of chef has resulted in menus to suit modern tastes. Smoked salmon and Chateaubriand steaks remain perennial favorites, but guests are now offered numerous other options: imaginative light sauces, fresh fruit, grills, seafood, salads, and even health-conscious dishes specially suggested by a consultant dietary physician. Desserts can be refreshing instead of creamy – a fan of fresh orange and grapefruit with ginger-flavored sorbet, or hot passion-fruit soufflé accompanied by its own coulis and ice cream. A stately hotel run in the grand manner, La Gavina still has much to offer today's more exacting and demanding travelers.

Opposite: an idyllic setting for a lavish breakfast on the bedroom terrace. Above: the bar, styled like a ship's cabin. Overleaf: the façade, floodlit at night.

HOSTAL DE LA GAVINA, plaza de la Rosaleda, 17248 S'Agaro, Girona. **Tel.** (72) 32 11 00. **Telex** 57132. **Fax** (72) 32 15 73. **Owner** José Ensesa. **Manager** Gustavo Jean-Mairet. **Open** Spring to fall. **Rooms** 74 (incl. 16 suites), all with bathroom (incl. wall shower and hairdrier), direct-dial phone, satellite TV with 7 video channels, piped music, minibar, some with airconditioning, electronic safe, 24-hr room service. **Facilities** Salons, bar, 3 restaurants, elevator, airconditioning, 2 conference rooms, seawater pool with cabins and terrace restaurant and bar, gymnasium, Finnish sauna, jacuzzi, hairdresser, esthéticienne, quiro-massagist-physiotherapist, UVA solarium, 2 tennis courts, 2 paddle tennis courts; 3 18-hole golf courses nearby. **Restrictions** No dogs in restaurant. **Terms** Deluxe. **Credit cards** All major. **Closed parking** Yes, paying. **Getting there** Madrid 717km, N II A2/A7 dir. France, exit 7 via Llagostera to Sant Feliú. Turn N. up coast road to S'Agaro. Signposted on R, out on a promontory. **Of local interest** Beach, Begur, Aigua Blava (modern parador), Aiguafreda, Sa Tuna. **Whole day expeditions** Ceramics in La Bisbal; Pals (medieval city); Figueras Dalí Museum; Barcelona (see p. 69); Empúries (Greek and Roman excavations); casino at Lloret de Mar. **Eating out** Mas de Torrent (see p. 61), Eldorado Petit (Sant Feliú de Guixols), El Bulli (Rosas), Mas Pau (see p. 59).

A proud tradition maintained

Taking internal flights round Spain makes good sense in a country large by European standards, where major cities are not yet linked by motorways, and which is divided by high mountain chains. The service between Madrid and Barcelona is rapid and efficient, and both airports are modern and well-organized. There were, moreover, plenty of metered taxis waiting outside the arrivals terminal in Barcelona.

A uniformed doorman welcomes you to the Ritz, which stands on one of Barcelona's main thoroughfares, the Gran Via de les Corts Catalanes. The first Ritz, opened by César Ritz in Paris in 1898, was a tremendously elaborate glittering palace. The Barcelona Ritz maintains the same proud traditions of service to guests, and luxurious comfort, though its architecture is a harbinger of the simpler flowing lines that became popular in the Twenties. It was opened in 1919.

The year before, César Ritz had died, a perfectionist who wore himself out in his successful attempt to revolutionize hotel-keeping by introducing fitted wardrobes, a private bathroom for every bedroom, plain walls which could constantly be repainted, elevators, and "the electricity" instead of gas lamps.

From the marble entrance hall twin staircases rise in graceful curves above an impressive doorway leading to a rotunda featuring fashionable "vitrines," and to the enormous oval pillared salon, lined with mirrors and embellished with palm trees. On its right, the stately, chandelier-hung Restaurante Diane is paneled in cream, blue, and white; the vast marble fireplace at one end provides a focal point. The original carpet is richly patterned in blue, pink, black, and gold. Downstairs is an intimate piano bar.

As the hotel was fully booked, I was given the bedroom portion of the Royal Suite – they showed me the separate sitting room, lined with gilded chairs, vast enough to hold court in. The king-sized bed, which promised a night's sleep of comfort and considerable splendor, stood in a brocade-canopied alcove on a raised dais. When the bed was turned down for me, a linen mat was very correctly placed beside it. The high-ceilinged room boasted a marble fireplace and a huge walk-in closet with private safe. The immense bathroom housed a step-down vast pink marble Roman-style bath of positively regal size.

At dinner I enjoyed a light meal of mixed salad, barbecue-grilled chicken, and *crema catalana* – a type of crème brulée; the menu also offered a good choice of more complex dishes. Breakfast in my room was beautifully and formally served, set out on a linen cloth; included were a selection of succulent mini-pastries and breads, freshly squeezed orange juice, an assortment of preserves, and a pot of fragrant coffee.

This is a well-run, high-quality hotel, both stately and friendly, of which César Ritz could have felt justly proud.

In the colonnaded splendor of the salon (opposite), afternoon tea is served (above).

HOTEL RITZ, Gran Via de les Corts Catalanes 668, 08010 Barcelona. **Tel.** (3) 318 52 00. **Telex** 52739. **Fax** (3) 318 01 48. **Owners** Husa Hotels. **General Manager** Luis Torres. **Open** All year. **Rooms** 161 (incl. 6 suites), all with bathroom (incl. stall shower, robes, and hairdrier), remote-controlled satellite TV, minibar, airconditioning, walk-in closet, safe, double-glazing, direct-dial phone, 24-hr. room service, 24–hr. concierge/house-keeping/valet service. **Facilities** Salon, bar, restaurant, 2 elevators, airconditioning, garden, giftshop/newsstand, multi-lingual staff, 8 conference rooms. Private limousine to airport/auto-rental/babysitting/secretarial service by arrangement. **Restrictions** No dogs. **Terms** Super-deluxe. **Credit cards** All major. **Closed parking** Yes, paying. **Getting there** Madrid 627km via N II A2/A7 motorway. Hotel signposted in town. Airport 12km. **Of local interest** Museum of Catalan Art, Picasso Museum, Fundación Miró, Barrio Gotico (old town), cathedral, placa de S. Jaume, placa del Rei, Barrio Sta María del Mar, Barceloneta and seafront, Las Ramblas, architect Gaudí's unfinished Sagrada Familia church, Parque Güell. **Whole day expeditions** Sitges, Torres; Montserrat (monastery with black Virgin); S. Cugat abbey (Romanesque cloister); Terrassa (textile museum, castle, churches); Vilafranca del Penedés; Torrent (see p. 61). **Eating out** Via Veneto, Beltxenea, Reno, La Dorada, Botafumeiro, Eldorado Petit, Azulete, La Balsa, Finisterre, etc.

An intriguing historic fortress

Gypsies used to live in the castle ruins on the steep mound above the city of Tortosa, until the Spanish government took over the site and repaired the impressive Knights Templar fortress. Comfortable bedrooms and a large pool were added, so transforming it into a fascinating place for visitors to stay.

I had wondered, when planning my first winter trip to Spain, how rugged historic stone buildings could possibly be made comfortable; would they be inhabited by spiders and unhappy echoes of past tragedies – or ghosts? I set off rather apprehensively, packing plenty of woolens. What actually awaited me were enchanting, un-spooky castles, luxuriously refurbished by talented architects into excellent hotels enlivened by imaginative decor, furnished in the best local textiles and leather, and equipped with spotless modern bathrooms. Cosily warm in winter, they are, as I discovered on later visits, refreshingly cool on hot summer days.

The steep driveway up into the Castillo de la Zuda passes through two gateways into a wide courtyard filled with oleanders. Through embrasures in the crenellated walls, cannon point out over the city and Ebro river, which gave its name to the whole country of Iberus or Iberia. From the terrace by the pool, you can see part of the old city walls and, beside you, the former gunpowder magazine, now a conference room. Its windows were cut obliquely into immensely thick walls to prevent stray sparks getting in.

The large forecourt is now a garden planted with rose bushes and pine trees. Marble columns scattered about were discovered during reconstruction of the castle. The original *zuda*, or well, for which the castle is named, is still there, covered by a metal grill.

My bedroom window provided spectacular views of the sun setting over the river and the mountains beyond. The bedroom had attractive rural furnishings: simple wooden shutters, carved closet doors of solid wood, lozenge-shaped, highly-polished red tiles on the floor, and bedcovers woven locally in natural wool striped in green, red, and gold.

Hors d'oeuvres included shrimps and mussels, meat balls and smoked ham, asparagus and delicious salty Manchego cheese. Veal escalope was tender, the desserts tempting. The arched undercroft beneath the lofty dining room houses a pleasant bar and a sitting room offering splendid views. Large, brightly coloured local rugs are spread on the tiled floor.

The city was occupied over the centuries by Greeks, Romans, Carthaginians, and Moors, so it is no surprise that its mid-14th-century cathedral was built on the site where first a Roman temple and then a Moorish mosque had stood. Today Tortosa is a busy modern town, and the main highway to the south passes conveniently close by. The castle is a comfortable and intriguing place to break one's journey, be it north or south.

Decorative wrought-iron gates guard the main entrance (opposite). Meals are served with style (above).

PARADOR DE TURISMO CASTILLO DE LA ZUDA, 43500 Tortosa, Tarragona. **Tel.** (77) 44 44 50. **Fax** (77) 44 44 58. **Owners** Spanish Government. **Manager** Manuel Esteban Hernandez. **Open** All year. **Rooms** 82, all with bathroom (incl. wall shower), direct-dial phone, minibar. **Facilities** Salon, bar, restaurant, elevator, pool with children's pool (closed in winter), gardens, 2 conference rooms. **Restrictions** No dogs. **Terms** Moderate. **Credit cards** All major. **Getting there** Madrid 540 km via N III to Valencia, A7. Parador signposted in town. **Of local interest** Cathedral, old town, market. **Whole day expeditions** Barcelona (see p. 69); beaches – ask at parador. **Eating out** Racó de Mig-Camí, other small local restaurants.

A princely residence

Anyone familiar with El Greco's painting of Toledo which hangs in the Metropolitan Museum of Art, New York, will instantly recognize the skyline, walls, bridge, and hillside castle as they drive up to this city. To appreciate its setting, almost encircled by two arms of the Tajo River's steep-sided gorge, with a massive wall completing the defenses, drive round the surrounding ring road, but cautiously; it is narrow and much traveled by speeding tourist coaches.

Since I wished to stay in a hotel from which I could stroll out to explore the city without the worry of looking for somewhere to park, I elected to stay in the Hostal del Cardenal, though there is also a modern parador high up overlooking Toledo, where you may request a room with a panoramic vista, and which you must certainly visit anyway for the view.

The Hostal stands in a lovely, leafy, Moorish garden just inside the city walls. Its shady trees overhang rivulets and small fountains, pools and pathways, framed by the towering crenellated battlements. You climb steeply upwards via a series of stairways and terraces – best to leave your luggage to fetch later with the help of a porter – and reach the final flower-filled level before the front door. Above the door is a stone escutcheon topped by a cardinal's hat – the arms of the Cardinal Lorenzana, owner of the mansion and archbishop of Toledo in the 18th century.

The restaurant is a favorite lunching and dining place for locals and visitors alike, and forms a wing at right-angles to the house, reached through the hotel's breakfast room. Downstairs is a tiny bar and upstairs a pillared and colorfully tiled dining room in which hearty local dishes are served: grills, stuffed partridge, suckling pig, and marzipan desserts. You can order à la carte, though the set menu is sensibly priced.

Inside the hotel there are more Moorish touches – blue tiles, inner courtyards – as well as some splendid 18th-century ceilings. A small sitting room was furnished with antiques, and several ancient studded chests lined the corridor leading to my room. Bedrooms are fairly small, but pleasantly furnished in traditional carved furniture, with wrought-iron fittings and lamps. Walls and floor were tiled, as was the bathroom.

Toledo was famous as a city of learning long before the Crusades. Arab, Christian, and Jewish scholars studied and translated Greek, Hebrew, and Arabic texts together, disseminating their scientific, religious, and philosophical ideas to the rest of Europe. Even today, the archbishop of Toledo is primate of all Spain.

NB Neither this hotel nor the steep streets of the city will suit anyone who finds steps a problem, though a pause to see the view over the city is certainly worth a detour.

The Hostal stands within the city's Moorish walls (above). Opposite: a quiet courtyard; the building's façade, seen from the terraced gardens; and a corner of the tiled restaurant.

HOSTAL DEL CARDENAL, paseo de Recaredo 24, 45004 Toledo. **Tel.** (25) 22 49 00. **Fax** (25) 22 29 91. **Owners** Inturisa S.A. **Manager** D. José Gonzalez Martín. **Open** All year. **Rooms** 27, all with bathroom (incl. wall shower), direct-dial phone, minibar, some with airconditioning. NB No TV. **Facilities** 2 salons, bar, restaurant, gardens, 2 conference rooms next door. **Restrictions** No dogs in restaurant. **Terms** Moderate. **Credit cards** All major. **Closed parking** No, but night guardian. Free but tip appropriate. **Getting there** Madrid 70km via N 401. Drive straight to main gate, turn R, follow walls round 2 traffic circles, then back up dual carriageway along walls, hotel sign on R. **Of local interest** Hospital de Santa Cruz museum, Santiago del Arrabal church, Puerta Nueva de Bisagra, Hospital de Tavera museum, Alcázar dungeons, Sto Cristo de la Luz church/mosque, cathedral, Judería, El Greco's house, Sto Tomé church with El Greco's *Burial of the Count of Orgaz*. **Whole day expeditions** Castles at Guadamur and Barcience; Talavera de la Reina potteries; Hospital de la Caridad, Illescas, with El Greco paintings; Orgaz and Tembleque main squares; Madrid (see pp. 47, 51); Chinchón (see p. 53). **Eating out** Chirón, Venta de Aires, Adolfo.

In La Mancha

In the heart of La Mancha, famed for the imaginary exploits of Cervantes' knightly hero Don Quixote, is the ancient town of Almagro. In October each year the fields which surround it are purple with autumn crocuses, from which is produced the saffron that tints paella rice its characteristic golden color. Saffron takes its name from the Arabic word for yellow: *asfar*. Since half a million flower stamens are needed to produce a kilo of saffron, it is understandably expensive.

In contrast with many Spanish towns crammed inside high walls on a hilltop, Almagro is a sprawling plain's city crossed by broad streets and with its own sleepy charm. Its parador echoes the town's character; it is a rambling building, entered through a wrought-iron gateway that leads into a wide courtyard. An ornamental pool reflects the bell-tower and massive main portal, in which is set an iron-studded door. The entry hall floor is made of pebbles laid to form a pattern. Inside this former Franciscan convent, built in 1596, are fourteen delightful courtyards, encircled by galleried double arcades with polished-tile corridors; each has its own variation on the theme of wells, fountains, rose gardens, trees, lawns, paths, or neatly raked gravel.

The whole parador has tremendous personality. The bar is a former storeroom with a bar-counter painted bright red. Tables are arranged around the 3-foot-wide wooden lids of gigantic pottery storage jars, whose bases rest 15 feet below on the floor of a lower story; just their shoulders emerge from the floor of the bar. Jars like these are still used in the region for storing its splendid Valdepeñas wines.

At the restaurant entrance there are heavy beams painted deep purple, green, white, and red in complex patterns. Food here is hearty and tasty. The local specialties are game and roast lamb, and you should also sample the aubergines or eggplants (*berenjenas*) which were originally introduced to this region by the Moors. The assorted dishes of hors d'oeuvres were as

always both intriguing and delicious, and the Valdepeñas wine smooth and full-bodied. The beamed room is packed with items to attract the interest of the diners: fascinating country antiques, ancient presses, painted tiles, and arrangements of dried grasses.

The bedrooms, which are fairly small, are trimmed with decorative tiles – dark blue in my modern bathroom – and have carved furniture. I had a glorious view of full-blown pink roses climbing up the courtyard wall.

A lady sitting in one of the corridors was making lace, her fingers a blur among flying bobbins. I bought some delicate snowflake-fine pieces, and listened to her fears that the craft will die out soon because the younger generation is unwilling to learn lacemaking.

You must not leave Almagro without visiting the main square, the plaza Mayor, dating from 1372. Like the square of Chinchón (see p. 53), it is sometimes used for bullfights. You should also see the 16th-century Corral de las Comedias theater, which resembles a square version of Shakespeare's Globe and is still in use.

Opposite: the unusual bar, with huge storage jars projecting through the floor, and a tastefully furnished bedroom. Above: a local lacemaker.

PARADOR DE TURISMO DE ALMAGRO, ronda de San Francisco, 13270 Almagro, Ciudad Real. **Tel.** (26) 86 01 00. **Fax** (26) 86 01 50. **Owners** Spanish Government. **Manager** José Muñoz Romera. **Open** All year. **Rooms** 55, all with bathroom (incl. wall shower), direct-dial phone, TV, airconditioning. **Facilities** Salon, bar, restaurant, airconditioning, pool (summer only), gardens, 3 conference rooms. NB No elevator. **Restrictions** No dogs. **Terms** Moderate. **Credit cards** All major. **Closed parking** Yes, free. **Getting there** Madrid 189km via N IV, turn off at Puerto Lápice dir. Ciudad Real, and again at Daimiel. Parador signposted in town. **Of local interest** Plaza Mayor with Corral de las Comedias theater; lacemakers. **Whole day expeditions** Valdepeñas (wine producers); Manchego cheeses (should be stamped and dated); Ciudad Real cathedral; San Clemente and Campo de Criptana villages, windmill; Belmonte castle; Lagunas de Ruidera lakes. **Eating out** Mesón El Corregidor.

High above the olive groves

The parador in Jaén occupies a classic setting for a castle, high on a hilltop above the city. It is engulfed by a sea of olive orchards which climb every slope of the rugged crags. Below lies the valley of the River Guadalquivír. On the skyline rise the mountains of the Sierra Morena and the Sierra Nevada.

The castle, reconstructed from the ruins of a 13th-century stronghold, succeeds in recreating the atmosphere of the original impregnable fortress. Its narrow corridors have small windows of colored glass, and lead into a series of vast, vaulted rooms. The main sitting room has armor, tapestries, and a giant fireplace. Another seating area is tucked into an angle of a monumental stone staircase that leads up inside the immensely thick walls; it too has an open hearth.

The bedrooms are protected by double glass doors from the wind that funnels down between the peaks; tiled balconies hang over the sheer drop below. Bedrooms are comfortable and pleasantly furnished in local fabrics. Bathrooms are attractively faced in pale gray marble. Breakfast was particularly good.

From the dining room windows you can gaze out at the hillside. The food was delicious, and after initially contemplating local partridge, a great regional specialty, I decided in the end on a garlic soup with big grapes floating in it – an apparently strange combination which in fact worked well – grilled swordfish which was juicily tender, and an Eastern-type dessert flavored with aniseed, honey, and almonds. The further south one drives the stronger the Moorish influence becomes. The road up to the parador winds between white-washed houses, and the wooden shutters throughout the hotel are pierced by star-shaped holes: it could be Morocco.

Jaén (pronounced Hi-en), nowadays a big modern city, has a fascinating history. Esteemed by the Romans for the nearby silver mines, it was later fortified by the Arabs, then captured from them on Saint Catalina's Day, 1246, by Ferdinand III. His Christian troops and their successors went on to withstand two more centuries of assaults on their heavily fortified eyrie.

From Jaén you can drive west to Córdoba – its Great Mosque is one of the wonders of the world and every visitor to this area should wander through its cool, dark forest of ancient pillars, topped with graceful double Moorish arches. Walk in its courtyard orange grove; explore Córdoba's flower-filled streets; eat across from the mosque at the cheerful Caballo Rojo (Red Horse) restaurant, and stay at its modern parador.

To the east is the outstandingly picturesque city of Ubeda, with its historic and equally enchanting parador. All around it colorful villages nestle in the mountain valleys.

The public rooms in the castle are of monumental proportions (opposite and above). The balconied bedrooms (overleaf) look out over extensive olive groves and mountain slopes.

PARADOR DE TURISMO CASTILLO DE SANTA CATALINA, 23000 Jaén. **Tel.** (53) 26 44 11. **Fax** (53) 22 39 30. **Owners** Spanish Government. **Manager** D. Antonio Romero Huete. **Open** All year. **Rooms** 45, all with bathroom (incl. wall shower), direct-dial phone, TV, minibar, airconditioning. **Facilities** 3 salons, 2 bars, 2 restaurants, elevator, airconditioning, pool, conference room. **Restrictions** No dogs. **Terms** Moderate. **Credit cards** All major. **Closed** **parking** No. **Getting there** Madrid 336km via N IV, turn off at Bailén. Parador signposted and visible from town. Avoid rush hour if possible. **Of local interest** Castle chapel, archaeological museum, Arab baths, cathedral. **Whole day expeditions** Córdoba; Ubeda; Baeza; Sierra de Cazorla; Cazorla; Alcalá la Real. **Eating out** Ask at hotel.

A home from home

If you want to explore Extremadura – the land from which many of the Conquistadors came – find out about Cádiz, or just spend a lazy holiday with barbecues by the pool and a view of chestnut orchards and hills, you should go to stay at the Finca Buen Vino just short of the Portuguese border, halfway between Lisbon and Seville.

As I drove up from Seville, I enjoyed the sights of the countryside. Eventually I turned as instructed between yellow pillars, and along a rough track, to my first view of this bewitching private house.

Finca Buen Vino is run by Sam and Jeannie Chesterton. Sam is a great-nephew of writer G.K. Chesterton, and is himself a writer. Jeannie's Cordon Bleu training helped her to run a restaurant in Hong Kong and an executive catering business in London.

When the Chestertons married, they came to live in Spain, where they are now busy raising their three young children. These occasionally make unscheduled appearances at dinnertime – only to be swiftly banished. Scheduled dinner guests may include relatives visiting from Scotland, local artists – whose paintings hang throughout the house – friends who have driven the 6½ hours down from Madrid, or the current au pair girl from New Zealand.

The house stands near an ancient spring, which never dries up even in the hottest summer. A Roman coin has been found in the grounds, and it was probably the Romans who planted the ancestors of the chestnut trees in the orchard, and ground the chestnuts to make flour.

There are wonderful views from all the windows, even the bathrooms, and bedrooms are decorated in pretty chintzes. The delicate hand-stencilled trim round the doors is the work of Sam and Jeannie. Downstairs, the Chinese yellow drawing room has a splendid English country-house feeling, thanks to the bequest by Jeannie's godmother of the contents of her southern-counties home. Antique wall panels came from a house in Madrid.

Breakfast is taken on a glassed-in terrace overlooking the wooded hills; lunch for those who wish it is often served beside the pool, dinner by candlelight. A canary sings sweetly, the roses climbing up the courtyard wall are from Kiftsgate in England, and the encircling slopes are smothered in wildflowers in spring. The Chestertons grow their own fruit and vegetables, and neighbors also often drop by laden with baskets of melons, tomatoes, grapes, figs, or green beans.

Sam and Jeannie Chesterton are a delightful couple with a gift for making guests so welcome that you feel as though you had known them for years. In view of its joyous accompaniment of small children and dogs, this is not a household for the starchily formal. For their candlelit dinner, however, everyone takes the trouble to change into something less relaxed than daytime sportswear.

Tulips decorate the terrace (above), roses from England the courtyard (opposite). The drawing room provides country-house comfort. Overleaf: dinner is elegantly set, the bedroom cosy and inviting, the views breathtaking.

FINCA BUEN VINO, Los Marines, 21293 Iluelva. **Tel.** and **fax** (55) 12 40 34. **Owners** Sam and Jeannie Chesterton. **Open** Feb.–mid-Aug.; mid-Sept.–mid-Dec. NB This is a private house, so all bookings must be made in advance. **Rooms** 3, 1 with en-suite, 2 with private bathroom opposite. Hairdrier, but no showers. **Facilities** Drawing room, dining room, conservatory, TV room, honesty bar, pool with terrace, gardens and extensive grounds. Tennis court planned. Collection from airport by arrangement. **Restrictions** None. **Terms** Moderate. **Credit cards** None; personal checks or cash only. **Closed parking** No. **Getting there** Madrid 534 km via Mérida, Zafra, Galaroza. Int. airport, Malaga, 310km; local, Seville 103km. Ask agent directions when booking. **Of local interest** Aracena caves, castle of the Knights Templar, mosque of Almonaster; local village summer fiestas, ceramics, basketwork, furniture. Ask hosts. **Whole day expeditions** Seville; Carmona; Zafra (churches and parador); Mérida (probably finest Roman remains in Spain, parador); Jerez de los Caballeros; Jerez de la Frontera/Cádiz (parador); Mazagón (parador, winter migratory birds).

Tradition in the Moorish style

This is a palatial, traditional grand hotel, built in the Moorish style, set in its own palm-tree-filled garden. Opened in 1929, it had been allowed latterly to run to seed, but happily is now being restored to its former glory. The staff are helpful, well-trained, and polite.

There is an impressive entrance hall – where an upmarket boutique sells fine Loewe leather goods – a beamed and tiled arched inner hall, and an ornate main stairway. At the heart of the hotel is a square marble courtyard, with wide, glassed-in arcades which have conversation groups of comfortable rattan armchairs, writing desks, and a bar. Palm-trees and flowers surround a central fountain. In summer, awnings pulled across at roof level cast striped shadows. The hotel is airconditioned, essential in the crushing, best-avoided heat of summer – visit in spring.

A wrought-iron gate leads into the restaurant, where chandeliers cascading with crystal droplets are suspended from the beamed ceiling. Lined with mirrors and acres of oil paintings, it is decorated with beautiful arrangements of fresh flowers, gilding, and statuary. Breakfast is lavish and formally served, with succulent pastries and fresh fruit; the dinner menu is international and suitably grand.

Upstairs, bedrooms are gradually being renovated and their richly inlaid marble floors reinstated. Be sure to ask for a room which has been refurbished, to avoid disappointment, or for a more spacious suite. The bathrooms are tiled and modern.

A trio of enormous reception rooms opening one into another extends along one side of the hotel. Seville's most prestigious social events are held amid the glittering luxury of their gold brocade and chandeliers.

Seville has wonderful parks and enchanting flowery patios off a maze of colorful back streets in the

Santa Cruz area. The university, once a tobacco factory, provided the setting for Bizet's *Carmen*. A pleasantly relaxing way to see the sights is by horse-drawn carriage. Settle the price before getting in.

The world-famous April Fiesta just after Holy Week is quintessential Spain. Girls proudly show off their brilliantly colored, many-layered frilled dresses and mantillas, and flower-decked streets are filled with processions of horsemen and carriages. Even if it is not fiesta time, you can enjoy a display of flamenco dancing. Avoid the many inferior tourist-traps by asking the hotel to arrange an outing for you.

The Hotel Alfonso XIII is centrally situated and provides the ideal base from which to explore Seville.

Sunlight stripes the marble courtyard (opposite) and brings to life the stained glass windows (above).

HOTEL ALFONSO XIII, San Fernando 2, 41004 Seville. **Tel.** (5) 422 28 50. **Telex** 72725. **Fax** (5) 421 60 33. **Owners** City corporation. **Managing company** Cigahotels. **Manager** Luis Fernandez Sauco. **Open** All year. **Rooms** 149 (incl. 19 suites), all with bathroom (incl. wall shower), direct-dial phone, TV, radio, minibar, airconditioning. **Facilities** Salon, bar, restaurant, elevator, airconditioning, pool, gardens, hairdresser, boutiques, 6 conference rooms. **Restrictions** No dogs. **Terms** Deluxe. **Credit cards** All major. **Closed parking** Yes, paying. **Getting there** Madrid 550km via N IV. Airport 13km, or Málaga, 217km. Follow signs for university next door. **Of local interest** Cathedral, Giralda, Archive of the Indies, Alcázar, Barrio de Santa Cruz, María Luisa Park, Museo de Bellas Artes, Calle de las Sierpes shopping, Holy Week and April Fiesta. **Whole day expeditions** Itálica (Roman ruins); Jerez (sherry producers); Cádiz; Carmona (see p. 87); Córdoba (Great Mosque). **Eating out** Egaña Oriza, San Marco, La Dorada.

Imaginative decor in a Roman citadel

It was the imaginative decor which particularly attracted me to this parador in the fascinating town of Carmona, not far from Seville. It has an imposing setting, perched on an escarpment site already ancient when the Romans came.

I entered Carmona through the Granada gateway, between massive twin Roman turrets, carefully avoiding a herd of goats clattering out to their pastures. The white houses in the winding cobbled streets have ornate wrought-iron window grills, and church towers can be glimpsed above their tiled roofs. Through a Moorish arch in the parador's massive stone walls, a wide cobbled courtyard stretches in front of a façade which looks more like a palace than a castle. Seen from the other side, however, its buttressed walls built into towering cliffs are suitably fortress-like. The entry hall is lofty, the inner courtyard has slender pillars topped with Moorish arches.

Throwing open my bedroom shutters I found vast, flat, December-brown plains, reaching in the far distance to mountains over which, later that evening, I saw a spectacular sunset.

A panel of delicate Moorish patterns on a bright blue background hung on my bedroom wall. There were chairs of crimson velvet, gray-painted bedheads carved with flowers lightly picked out in green and gold, bedcovers patterned in a subtle leafy swirl, and Moroccan rugs on the tiled floor. The bathroom of pale gray marble was inset with Moorish tiles.

The bar vividly reminded me of my years in the Middle East; through ceiling insets of brightly colored glass, light filtered on to brass tables and low leather chairs. The dining room had crystal lanterns and a high vaulted ceiling with brick ribs. Seated by the window, I looked down to a sparkling pool edged with tiled pavilions, surrounded by gardens filled with orange trees, oleanders, and bougainvillea, among which small birds flitted. Beyond, white egrets stalked majestically on a river bank.

After a complimentary glass of sherry and some startlingly good local olives and salted almonds, I chose a typical dish of spinach with chick peas, lightly flavored with cumin; red mullet delicately battered and fried, like Japanese tempura; and a cake-like dessert which included pine nuts. In the morning the breakfast table groaned under mounds of delicious breads, cakes, pastries, fresh fruits, home-made preserves, and cold cuts. Coffee was accompanied by milk whipped to a froth – the parador has an excellent chef.

The town is full of churches, mosaic pavements, and Roman tombs, and is well worth exploring. Although Don Pedro, after whom the castle is named, has a history worthy of the Brothers Grimm, the parador is friendly and welcoming – a most pleasant and convenient base for visiting Seville or Córdoba.

Opposite: the Moorish-tiled courtyard patio – perfect for pre-lunch drinks. Above: light filters into the bar through colored glass in the ceiling. Overleaf: the restaurant windows overlook the pool and surrounding countryside.

PARADOR DE TURISMO ALCÁZAR DEL REY DON PEDRO, Alcázar, 41410 Carmona, Seville. **Tel.** (5) 414 10 10. **Telex** 72992. **Fax** (5) 414 17 12. **Owners** Spanish Government. **Manager** Benito Montañés Sierra. **Open** All year. **Rooms** 65, all with bathroom (incl. wall shower), direct-dial phone, TV, radio, minibar. **Facilities** Salon, bar, restaurant, elevator, pool, terraces and patios, 2 conference rooms. **Restrictions** No dogs. **Terms** Expensive. **Credit cards** All major. **Closed parking** Inside parador wall. **Getting there** Madrid 503km via N IV; Seville airport 17km. **Of local interest** Local churches, mosaic pavements, Roman necropolis. **Whole day expeditions** Seville (see p. 85); Córdoba. **Eating out** Ask at parador about small local places.

The ideal hotel in a perfect setting

If I could return to only one hotel in Spain, this would be it. La Bobadilla is the epitome of countryside excellence: luxuriously comfortable, tastefully furnished, with wonderful food, set in beautiful surroundings, with a well-equipped health and beauty complex, and considerate, polite, friendly, multilingual, highly trained staff. It provides tennis courts, horse-back riding, a pool to loll by, and southern Spain's most spectacular cities within easy reach. This is the ideal spot to honeymoon, to unwind after your classical concert tour, to hold a relaxed top-level discussion on that next multimillion-dollar decision, or simply to have a memorable holiday.

The three-kilometer drive winds slowly upwards through olive trees silver-gray against the red earth. After parking, you follow a path into what seems to be a small village square, with tall chapel bell-tower, tubs of flowers and trees, a medley of balconies and tiled roof-tops, and central fountain. The hotel complex meanders across the hillside, linked by polished tiled corridors, stairways, and patios with fountains.

A black-jacketed manager worthy of the Savoy greets you in the marble-floored, Moorish-arched entrance hall. Conducted to my suite, I found it elegantly decorated with the same loving care as a private house. The king-sized bed, set into a deep brick surround, was flanked by bedside lamps converted from antique candlesticks with snuffers. There was an ancient pine desk, a carved and gilded mirror, and a separate sitting area with sofa and coffee table. The bathroom was luxurious.

Other suites have open hearth, four-poster, dining table, their own patios, and steps up to a private rooftop sun-terrace. The suite preferred by Spain's king and queen is even larger, in a tower, convenient for security, and with splendid views over the surrounding countryside.

Polished brass and huge arrangements of flowers give a welcoming air to the spacious, comfortable bar. The vast pool is free-form and edged with palm trees and an 18-hole golf course is planned.

I indulged myself with the full gourmet menu in "La Finca" restaurant. Delicate and beautifully presented, it consisted of a wisp of smoked salmon accompanied by a confection of courgettes, followed by emerald-green broccoli soup, fish terrine with lobster sauce, a sharply refreshing lemon sorbet, quail garnished with foie gras, a selection of farm cheeses, and a gratin of wild blueberries. Coffee arrived with a silver bon-bon dish of truffles. The breakfast buffet next morning was the finest I have seen. Top-quality Spanish dishes are served in the less formal "El Cortijo" restaurant-bar.

Although Michelin have awarded only one niggardly star, La Bobadilla's food and comfort was definitely in the category of "vaut le voyage" ("worth a special journey").

Guests can relax in the courtyard's shaded arcades or in the cool, elegant sitting room (opposite). Above: a trompe l'oeil dessert. Overleaf: the hotel complex in its lovely hillside setting.

HOTEL LA BOBADILLA, Finca la Bobadilla, apartado 52, 18300 Loja, Granada. **Tel.** (58) 32 18 61. **Telex** 78732. **Fax** (58) 32 18 10. **Owner** Rudolf Karl Staab. **Manager** Juan Sendra Farré. **Open** All year. **Rooms** 62, all with bathroom (incl. tub and shower stall), direct-dial phone, satellite TV, radio on request, airconditioning, 24-hr. room service, laundry/dry cleaning/pressing. **Facilities** Salon, 2 bars (1 summer only), 2 restaurants, pool, health and beauty complex with indoor plunge pool, gardens, 2 conference rooms, audio-visual/secretarial/simultaneous translation services. Chapel organ recital/concert/flamenco entertainment by arrangement. Hire of minibus/coach/chauffeured limousine with guide/helicopter/private jet by arrangement. Riding, shooting by arrangement. 2 tennis courts. 9-hole golf planned. NB No elevator. **Restrictions** No dogs in restaurant. **Terms** Super-deluxe. **Credit cards** All major. **Closed parking** No, but patrolled. **Getting there** Madrid 487km via N IV, Granada, Málaga road turn off km 502 dir. Seville, through Salinas, turn towards Rute; after 3km watch for hotel gate on R. Local airport, Granada, 57km; int. airport, Málaga, 71km. **Of local interest** Riding/tennis/shooting by arrangement. **Whole day expeditions** Seville (see p. 85); Granada (see p. 95); Córdoba. **Eating out** No.

At the heart of the Alhambra

"While the city below pants with the noontide heat . . . the delicate airs from the Sierra Nevada play through these lofty halls, bringing with them the sweetness of the surrounding gardens . . . the ear is lulled by the rustling of groves and the murmur of running streams." So wrote Washington Irving in his *Tales from the Alhambra* (1832), describing the Moorish hilltop fortress which remains as enchanting today. He stayed for several months in the apartments of the Governor of the Alhambra, and later wrote the charming book that was to become essential reading for the would-be visitor.

Its lofty, rose-red sandstone walls gave the Alhambra its name – "al-Hamra," the red, in Arabic. At the peak of the Moorish conquest 40,000 people lived inside these walls. You approach through a shady wood; once inside, the Casa Real is on your left, a series of rooms with delicate slender pillars, ceilings carved into hanging stalactites, pools, fountains, and the incomparable Court of the Lions. When you have walked through all the palace rooms, leave plenty of time to enjoy the lovely terraced gardens.

There are further towers and gardens to explore outside the palace itself, as well as the massive Renaissance palace built by Charles V, containing a fine arts and an Hispano-Moorish museum. There is also a small street of restaurants and tourist shops. Outside the walls, looking down on the Alhambra, stands the Generalife Palace with its magnificent, peaceful gardens. The pathway to the Palace is beside the entrance to the 15th-century Convent of San Francisco, probably the busiest parador in all Spain. To reach the parador from Granada, head uphill, following signs and, on arriving, ask the porter to unlock the gates to the parador's parking area.

You must book literally months in advance to stay here. The central courtyard is glorious, floored in patterned pebbles, with a tall cypress in one corner, and perfumed with orange blossom, jasmine, and roses. The water trickling over the central fountain cools the air, and murmurs along sunken channels at the courtyard's edge, where rocking chairs and cushioned benches invite one to linger in the shady arcades. Leading from the courtyard is a Moorish pavilion.

My small, simple bedroom had carved furniture and a good modern bathroom well-furnished with toiletries. There were pleasant views from the window over the gardens. The large public rooms contain interesting antiques. The staff have a slightly harrassed air, due to year-long full occupancy and the many groups arriving for meals. But the great advantage of staying in the parador San Francisco is that you are right at the heart of the Alhambra, poised to explore it on foot, to see it in the dewy early morning or, magically, by moonlight.

Above: an intriguing antique door knocker. Opposite: the enchanting central courtyard. Overleaf: the epitome of Southern Spain – ripe oranges among glossy leaves.

PARADOR DE TURISMO DE SAN FRANCISCO, real de la Alhambra, 18009 Granada. **Tel.** (58) 22 14 40. **Telex** 78792. **Fax** (58) 22 22 64. **Owners** Spanish Government. **Manager** J. A. Fernandez Aladro. **Open** All year. **Rooms** 39, all with bathroom (incl. wall shower), direct-dial phone, TV, minibar, airconditioning. **Facilities** Salon, bar, restaurant, airconditioning, gardens, 1 conference room. NB No elevator. **Terms** Expensive. **Credit cards** All major. **Restrictions** No dogs. **Closed parking** Yes, paying. **Getting there** From Madrid 430km via N IV, turn off dir. Jaén, Granada. Signposted in town. Int. airport, Málaga, 127km, local airport Granada, 17km. **Of local interest** Alhambra, Alcázar, Generalife gardens, palace of Charles V with art/Hispano-Moorish museums (NB Buy tickets near main gate); in town: cathedral, royal chapel. **Whole day expeditions** Córdoba (Great Mosque); Seville (see p. 85); Jaén/Ubeda (see p. 77); Ronda. **Eating out** Baroca, Cunini, Ruta del Veleta, Sevilla.